ROB DE JONGH

Genesis

Food for thought in the Old Testament series

WOODLAND PRESS

First published by Woodland Press Ltd 2021

Copyright © 2021 by Rob de Jongh

All rights reserved. No part of this publication may be reproduced, stored or transmitted in any form or by any means, electronic, mechanical, photocopying, recording, scanning, or otherwise without written permission from the publisher. It is illegal to copy this book, post it to a website, or distribute it by any other means without permission.

Scripture quotations from the Authorized (King James) Version. Rights in the Authorized Version in the United Kingdom are vested in the Crown. Reproduced by permission of the Crown's patentee, Cambridge University Press.

Contributions by Peter L. Forbes used by kind permission.

First edition

ISBN: 978-1-913699-04-8

This book was professionally typeset on Reedsy. Find out more at reedsy.com

Contents

Introduction	vii
Reading with your family	viii
Leading discussion groups	viii
Preparing a Bible talk or lecture	viii
Preparing a sermon or exhortation	ix
Aiding personal Bible study	ix
How not to use this book!	ix
Food for thought in Genesis	xi
Genesis 1	1
How it all began: Eden the source of life	1
Genesis 2	5
The event that formed the earth	5
Genesis 3	9
Did the serpent lie, or was Eve deceived?	9
Genesis 4	14
How to combat sin from within	14
Genesis 5	17
What is God's image and likeness?	17
Genesis 6	20
The eyes of the LORD	20
Genesis 7	23
How did all the animals fit on the Ark?	23
Genesis 8	25
The evidence of the flood beneath our feet	25
Genesis 9	27

Never again!	27
Genesis 10	31
Noah's Grandsons	31
Genesis 11	33
Be fruitful, and multiply, and replenish the earth	33
Genesis 12	36
Babel, the promises, and you	36
Genesis 13	41
Bible questions	41
Genesis 14	43
Led by God, or led by … ?	43
Genesis 15	49
Abram: The father of salvation by faith	49
Abram's Amorite Allies	50
Genesis 16	52
Abram hearkened to the voice of Sarai	52
Genesis 17	56
Abraham's Circumcision Implementation Committee (ACIC)	56
Food for thought	59
Genesis 18	60
Abraham and Lot: The Godly and worldly household	60
Genesis 19	64
Comparing Lot with Abraham	64
Genesis 20	67
Why did Abraham move?	67
Genesis 21	69
Who do we listen to?	69
Genesis 22	73
The place I will show you	73
Genesis 23	77

The parable of Abraham's field	77
Genesis 24	80
Isaac's long wait	80
Genesis 25	83
Esau the profane person	83
Genesis 26	86
Isaac's bodyguard	86
Genesis 27	88
He found no place of repentance	88
Genesis 28	92
Does it matter whom we marry?	92
Genesis 29	96
Finding a wife at the well	96
Genesis 30	100
The rivalry of Rachel and Leah explained	100
Genesis 31	103
God doesn't forget His promises	103
The countenance of Laban	104
Genesis 32	106
Jacob's struggle	106
Genesis 33	109
Brothers reunited and still apart	109
Genesis 34	112
Be ye separate, saith the Lord	112
Genesis 35	115
Bible echoes	115
The beginning of idolatry - Rachel's mistake	115
Genesis 36	118
Brothers of promise	118
Genesis 37	121
Open rebuke is better than concealed hatred	121

Genesis 38	125
Judah, the prodigal son	125
Genesis 39	127
Being allied with those who had the promises	127
Genesis 40	129
Extraordinary dreams for ordinary people	129
Genesis 41	132
Faith is the substance of things hoped for	132
Genesis 42	135
Unstable as water	135
Genesis 43	138
The sun, moon and stars	138
Genesis 44	142
Judah, the son who returned	142
Genesis 45	146
Joseph - a pattern of salvation in Jesus Christ	146
Genesis 46	149
The Mystery of the Missing Traveler	149
Genesis 47	151
I will multiply you exceedingly	151
Genesis 48	154
The extra portion	154
Genesis 49	158
The prophecies of Jacob	158
Genesis 50	161
Bring forth My armies	161
Epilogue	164
Other books in the series	166
About the Author	168

Introduction

When Jesus taught us to pray "give us today our daily bread", he wasn't talking about food, but the word of God. He said:

Man shall not live by bread alone, but by every word of God.

When Jesus met Peter after his resurrection and told Peter to feed the believers, he didn't mean with fish, but with the word of God:

So when they had dined, Jesus saith to Simon Peter, Simon, son of Jonas, lovest thou me more than these? He saith unto him, Yea, Lord; thou knowest that I love thee. He saith unto him, Feed my lambs.

Finding time to read the word of God can be difficult, and teaching it to others can seem an impossible task. Many of us simply *find ourselves* teaching the Bible, either at home to our life partner, or to our children, or as lay teachers or ministers or group leaders, without any training or resources.

Using the *Food for Thought in the Old Testament* series gives you a framework of Bible thoughts for each chapter of the Bible, allowing you to start discussion, create Bible talks and sermons, or simply to meditate on or dig deeper in your own study.

Reading with your family

If you are reading a chapter of the Bible at home with your family, first choose a chapter and read it together, preferably reading out loud (perhaps in sections of 2, 5 or 10 verses each) so that everyone gets a chance to join in. You can then find the relevant chapter in *Food for Thought in Genesis* and read one or more of the thoughts for that chapter. When you encounter a Bible reference, ask someone to turn it up and read it. Once you have finished, there may be questions in the text to answer, or the passage may have provided *food for thought* for further discussion.

Leading discussion groups

If you are leading a Bible discussion group, you could start by reading a chapter of the Bible around the group, followed by your presenting a short introduction of the chapter based on the relevant section of *Food for Thought in Genesis*. Once that is done, open up the group for discussion about any topics raised by the Bible chapter or in your introductory thoughts.

Preparing a Bible talk or lecture

If you are preparing a Bible talk or lecture, *Food for Thought in Genesis* can be used to piece your talk together using several sections of the book, or several books in the series. For example, for a character study on Abraham, use the eBook search feature or paperback index to list any sections including references to "Abraham" or "Abram". Piece together any sections that you think go well together, then read those sections and follow the Bible references in your Bible. Finally, write your discoveries down in your own words and practice at least once before presenting them.

Preparing a sermon or exhortation

For a talk/sermon or more motivational style thought, start with a topic from the contents list at the start of the book. Focus on the personal questions thrown up by that section, and spend time exploring what the Bible characters in that section were feeling, based on what we are told in the Bible chapter and any references provided in this book. Read out plenty of Scripture during your talk to illuminate what that character was like and what they went through.

Aiding personal Bible study

For your own personal Bible study, it is often helpful to start somewhere (anywhere is better than nowhere!) and follow where the path leads. *Food for Thought in Genesis* can help with this by providing many links to related Bible passages. Any of these will be well worth looking at to see how they relate to the partner passage in Genesis. Once you have two or more related passages, read over the context of each in your Bible and see what questions and conclusions jump out. Now follow other referenced passages out of those chapters, and so on.

How not to use this book!

This book series is not an explanation of the whole Old Testament. To do that would take a million pages. Many people have foolishly tried to create books like that, and failed. Reference works on the Bible are seldomly productive for Bible students, since they can stifle your ability to read the Word and make your own conclusions based on what you read.

Remember what we started the introduction with? The Bible is for food, not just for knowledge. Jesus asked Peter to feed, not people, but lambs and sheep. In other words, the Bible text is to be eaten, chewed over, and meditated on, in a similar way to how sheep chew over their food.

Rumination is the key to understanding the Old Testament.

This book is a collection of starting points, one or more for each chapter of Genesis. May God bless you as you step off from these onto your own journey through the scriptures.

Food for thought in Genesis

In the beginning God created the heaven and the earth.

So begins the Bible and the book of Genesis. It is not just the beginning of the book, but the beginning of the world. In the book of Genesis we look through the eyes of the Almighty Creator as He brings our marvelous world to life, shapes it out of a formless planet, creates the beasts of the field and the birds of the air, and creates mankind on the sixth day.

By following key moments in the lives of the first humans to set foot on our earth, we learn the most basic and important lessons our creator has to teach us. Through Adam and Eve we learn to obey, and the consequences of disobedience. Through Cain and Abel we learn about jealousy and the consequences of not developing a conscience. Through Noah we learn that there is good and evil, and that God will not allow evil to triumph. Through Abraham and Sarah we learn how to be separate from the evil of the world around us, and how to obtain salvation by faith in God's promises.

The book of Genesis is the foundation of the Bible, and can be the foundation for our lives too.

In the new testament the characters of Genesis are referred to again and again, from Paul using Adam and Eve as a pattern for faithful marriage and conduct in the congregation of believers, to Jesus who referred to his Father as "the God of Abraham, Isaac and Jacob". We see that Genesis is more than just a history of the start of the human race, it is the foundation for salvation.

It is by faith that we are saved, a gift of God, and this is based on one verse in the Old Testament that stands out, perhaps, above all others:

> *For what saith the scripture? Abraham believed God, and it was counted unto him for righteousness. (Rom 4:3)*

By looking into the life of Abraham and others, we may find the key to salvation that they found first in those ancient days. Abraham is the father of those who live by faith, and by this same faith we also may be saved.

> *Know ye therefore that they which are of faith, the same are the children of Abraham. And the scripture, foreseeing that God would justify the heathen through faith, preached before the gospel unto Abraham, saying, In thee shall all nations be blessed. So then they which be of faith are blessed with faithful Abraham. (Gal 3:7-9)*

Genesis 1

How it all began: Eden the source of life

In Genesis chapter 1 it is clear that God made a few of every fish and bird, then commanded them to spread across the globe, filling the sea and sky. In other words, life started somewhere and spread, just as it did with the land dwelling animals and people. See the following extract from the chapter:

> And God said, Let the waters bring forth abundantly the moving creature that hath life, and fowl that may fly above the earth in the open firmament of heaven. And God created great whales, and every living creature that moveth, which the waters brought forth abundantly, after their kind, and every winged fowl after his kind: and God saw that it was good. **And God blessed them, saying, Be fruitful, and multiply, and fill the waters in the seas, and let fowl multiply in the earth.** And the evening and the morning were the fifth day. (Gen 1:20-23)

How can we be sure that's correct? After all, the passage says God created them, not how many of each He created. It is clear that there were not many, because He commanded them to multiply — but we can't know how few, can we?

Actually, we can, because God commanded the same thing to mankind as He did to the fish and birds. Here God is speaking with Adam and Eve - one male and one female of the human species:

> *And God blessed them, and God said unto them,* **Be fruitful, and multiply, and replenish the earth***, and subdue it: and have dominion over the fish of the sea, and over the fowl of the air, and over every living thing that moveth upon the earth. (Gen 1:28)*

So by comparing two phrases that are the same, the Bible links itself. We have highlighted the phrase in **bold**, as we do throughout the *Food for thought in the Old Testament Series*. This is the first lesson of the first chapter of the first book of the Bible. In order for the Word of God to conceive life in you and me, for that word to come alive and explain itself, we need two of every kind. In other words, we need two verses that match and compliment one another, where the one explains the other. This is how the Bible reveals its message.

Then in chapter 2 we take a step back and find out that all this creating actually happened in the garden of Eden itself. There were presumably no animals created outside that Garden, or else Adam wouldn't have been able to name them:

> *And the LORD God said, It is not good that the man should be alone; I will make him an help meet for him. And out of the ground the LORD God formed every beast of the field, and every fowl of the air; and brought them unto Adam to see what he would call them: and whatsoever Adam called every living creature, that was the name thereof. And Adam gave names to all cattle, and to the fowl of the air, and to every beast of the field; but for Adam there was not found an help meet for him. (Gen 2:18-20)*

Notice that it was in the garden that God created the beasts and the fowl - so it was from there that they needed to spread out in order to fill the earth. There would be no reason to create more than two of any species.

So is this the same with the plants? Possibly, because the record seems to make the point that both rain and mankind were needed for plants to flourish, and mankind were only there in the garden:

> *These are the generations of the heavens and of the earth when they were created, in the day that the LORD God made the earth and the heavens, And every plant of the field before it was in the earth, and every herb of the field before it grew: for the LORD God had not caused it to rain upon the earth, and there was not a man to till the ground. (Gen 2:4-5)*

In fact, the rain didn't come until much later — in Noah's time — and we know that plants can't grow without rain. Except that, apparently starting here in the garden, there was a mist:

> *But there went up a mist from the earth, and watered the whole face of the ground. (Gen 2:6)*

Which is written in the context of God planting a garden. The garden of Eden:

> *And **the LORD God planted a garden eastward in Eden**; and there he put the man whom he had formed. And out of the ground made the LORD God to grow every tree that is pleasant to the sight, and good for food; the tree of life also in the midst of the garden, and the tree of knowledge of good and evil. (Gen 2:8-9)*

So it seems from the way these verses focus on Eden, that plants too were started there and by carrying seed they needed to spread out from that place. Even water itself started in Eden and spread out from there:

> *And a river went out of Eden to water the garden; and from thence it was parted, and became into four heads. (Gen 2:10)*

So the picture in Genesis is of all life starting in, or near, Eden, and spreading outwards gradually. The fish and birds would spread quickly, taking other smaller organisms and plant seeds with them wherever they went. And mankind and land animals would follow more slowly in relation to how slowly their reproductive cycle took. This explains how at the time of Noah all species were nearby enough to climb into the ark. And why God designed most plant seeds to be transported by birds, beasts, and rivers.

Food for thought

v1 - In the new testament both Mark 1:1 and John 1:1 echo language similar to this creation account in their gospel, highlighting the fact that the whole creation activity centres around God's plan of redemption in Jesus.

v26 - Whereas Adam was created in the image and likeness of God, Adam's children were in his image and likeness (Genesis 5:3) - what a contrast!

Genesis 2

The event that formed the earth

> *And a river went out of Eden to water the garden; and from thence it was parted, and became into four heads. The name of the first is Pison: that is it which compasseth the whole land of Havilah, where there is gold; And the gold of that land is good: there is bdellium and the onyx stone. And the name of the second river is Gihon: the same is it that compasseth the whole land of Ethiopia. And the name of the third river is Hiddekel: that is it which goeth toward the east of Assyria. And the fourth river is Euphrates. (Gen 2:10-14)*

It is impossible today to find rivers that start at the same source and end up in both Ethiopia and Assyria (modern day Iraq). So how should we understand what is being recorded here? Remember that this record is from before the flood, and it was at the time of the flood that enormous amounts of water came from heaven and from deep reservoirs in the earth:

> *In the six hundredth year of Noah's life, in the second month, the seventeenth day of the month, the same day were all the fountains*

of the great deep broken up, and the windows of heaven were opened. (Gen 7:11)

So before this event, while that water was not on the earth, but stored above and below it, there would have been far more land exposed. Presumably the Mediterranean Sea, Red Sea and Persian Gulf were not in existence so that there was an uninterrupted land mass right from Africa to China.

The land mass as we know it now was shaped by hundreds of meters of sedimentary deposits that were laid down as the flood waters dried. We know this because the word used in Genesis 7 "broken up" mean something rather more violent and catastrophic. We can find this out by looking at the Hebrew language which the Old Testament was originally written in. This is easier than it sounds. In the year 1890 James Strong published an index of every word in the King James version of the Bible. The wonderful thing about this index is that he gave each word a number relating to the Hebrew word that the English is translated from.

So for example, in our case "broken up" has Hebrew number 1234 - an easy one to remember! If we then go to the index of Hebrew numbers, we can find every use of that original Hebrew word in the whole Old Testament.

When we look at this, we can get a totally accurate flavour of what that word really meant when it was written. Our word, 1234, is found in the following passages:

*And Moses stretched out his hand over the sea; and the LORD caused the sea to go back by a strong east wind all that night, and made the sea dry land, and the waters were **divided**. (Exo 14:21)*
And he turned back, and looked on them, and cursed them in the name of the LORD. And there came forth two she bears out of

the wood, and **tare** forty and two children of them. (2Ki 2:24)

Whoso removeth stones shall be hurt therewith; and he that **cleaveth** wood shall be endangered thereby. (Ecc 10:9)

This is just a selection, with each occurrence of the word put in bold text. What idea do these three words give you of the earth at the time of Noah, when the fountains of the deep were broken up? Divided like the red sea. Torn or mauled like the bears who killed forty two people. Split like wood under an Axe.

The idea of the word is one of violent splitting or tearing, and that is what happened to the ground of the earth when it split apart violently and huge geysers of pressurised water burst forth. The volume of water was incredible, and the mud, sand, stone and minerals that came with it was equally huge. This formed the blanket of sediment that we now see all over the earth, and which changed it forever.

It is by carefully and prayerfully looking at what the word of God really says, and by resisting the urge to imagine it says what it does not, that we find answers to all the questions that it poses to us. We can then test those answers against other verses in the Bible to see if they hold true, and in this particular case, we can look at the natural world around us to see that, indeed, what we see is consistent with what we have found.

Food for thought

v7 - In John 6:63 Jesus says that his words are "spirit and life" echoing what we are told about the bringing of Adam to life. The word of God is as powerful in bringing to life (for us) as when God brought the clay to life (with Adam).

v16 - The command from God in the Garden of Eden was the first test of faith. Adam and Eve knew that God existed. They had to believe that he would keep His word. That is what faith is – believing God is reliable. See Romans 4:21.

Genesis 3

Did the serpent lie, or was Eve deceived?

Some of what the serpent says is correct, and some isn't. In Gen 3:22 God Himself says that upon eating of the tree, Adam and Eve became "as one of us", in other words, as the angels, having a conscience of good and evil.

> And the LORD God said, Behold, **the man is become as one of us, to know good and evil:** and now, lest he put forth his hand, and take also of the tree of life, and eat, and live for ever: (Gen 3:22)

This is what the serpent had said:

> For God doth know that in the day ye eat thereof, then your eyes shall be opened, and **ye shall be as gods, knowing good and evil.** (Gen 3:5)

So this part was true. The other part appears to be a blatant lie:

> And the serpent said unto the woman, **Ye shall not surely die:**

(Gen 3:4)

This appears to be a direct contradiction to what God had said to Adam when He forbade eating of the tree:

> *And the LORD God commanded the man, saying, Of every tree of the garden thou mayest freely eat: But of the tree of the knowledge of good and evil, thou shalt not eat of it:* ***for in the day that thou eatest thereof thou shalt surely die.*** *(Gen 2:16-17)*

Even the wording is the same in the two phrases, as if to say that the serpent quoted God but deliberately contradicted it.

But two questions come up. One, the fact that Adam didn't die, not for another nine hundred or more years. Second, that Adam could have reached out and eaten of the tree of life, and then he would have lived:

> *And the LORD God said, Behold, the man is become as one of us, to know good and evil:* ***and now, lest he put forth his hand, and take also of the tree of life, and eat, and live for ever: Therefore the LORD God sent him forth from the garden of Eden,*** *to till the ground from whence he was taken. (Gen 3:22-23)*

So what the serpent is saying is partly true, and the parts that appear to be a total lie, are also partly true. The serpent could indeed have said these words with the emphasis on "surely", as follows:

> *And the serpent said unto the woman, Ye shall not* surely *die...*

Did he know, as the angels of God did, that the tree of life was there in the garden, freely available? Was he actually reasoning upon the facts as he had them, and coming to a conclusion? It's quite possible that he was doing so.

Now, the Bible is internally consistent. If you discover something in one place, if it is true, then it will not be contradicted elsewhere. So if this point about the serpent is true, we can test it against the rest of scripture. Is the serpent elsewhere accused of directly lying?

Let's see first of all what God says when He confronts Adam, Eve and the serpent about what has happened:

> *And the LORD God said unto the serpent, Because thou hast done this, thou art cursed above all cattle, and above every beast of the field; upon thy belly shalt thou go, and dust shalt thou eat all the days of thy life: (Gen 3:14)*

Notice that God doesn't accuse the serpent of lying. He says "because you have done this". Also in the previous words Eve doesn't accuse the serpent of lying:

> *And the LORD God said unto the woman, What is this that thou hast done? And the woman said, The serpent beguiled me, and I did eat. (Gen 3:13)*

Think about this phrase, and see how precise we can trust the words of the Bible to be: "The serpent beguiled me".

If I said to you "that money in the till beguiled me, and I took it", where would you place the blame? The blame would be on me, wouldn't it? And if I said "my friend lied to me and I took the money", you might place most of the blame on the friend. The thing is that the Bible is precise in its wording, which is important because, if it weren't, it would be open to anyone interpreting it however they liked.

Here is the New Testament commentary on these events. Notice how precisely the writer of the letter to the Corinthians uses the Old Testament text:

> *But I fear, lest by any means, as the serpent beguiled Eve through his subtilty, so your minds should be corrupted from the simplicity that is in Christ. (2Co 11:3)*

Here it links the lesson of Genesis 3 we have been talking about, with the life of the Christian. Again it uses the words "subtilty" and "beguiled". The point that is being made is that there does not need to be a blatant lie to deceive us — we can be quite easily deceived by leaving behind the simplicity of what God has told us, and by instead building other inadequate things onto it. By looking at precisely what the serpent said, we can gain an idea of how this might happen to us.

Eve should have stuck with the simple commandment to "not eat of it", and moved away from the serpent if what he was saying seemed to contradict a clear commandment from God.

So the lesson is that it is possible to be deceived even if there is no lying involved. Being deceived is something that happens within the mind of the person themselves, and it is the responsibility of each one of us to guard against it. Being deceived can happen because of lack of knowledge, or by too much knowledge, or by incorrect reasoning on the knowledge we have.

The answer to the question posed in the title of this chapter is given to us in the New Testament. Here, as we have already discovered, the responsibility for being deceived is placed squarely at the feet of Eve:

> *And Adam was not deceived, but the woman being deceived was in the transgression. (1Ti 2:14)*

Food for thought

v1 - Nakedness passes into Biblical use as an indicator of being astray from God. The word translated "subtil" (Strongs Hebrew number 06175) is closely related to the word translated as "naked" (Strongs Hebrew number 06174) in Gen 2:25.

v6 - The mental process that eve went through, from seeing to taking, is reflected in the behaviour of Achan (see Josh 7:21) and David (see 2Sam 11:2-4) highlighting that Eve's problem is common to all mankind.

v10 - When Adam and Eve were afraid and hid they showed the behaviour of anyone who views God with terror. Jesus drew on this – Matt 25:25 – when he talks of the man who hid his talent in the ground. Are we terrified of God or full of awe?

Genesis 4

How to combat sin from within

The book of Genesis is introducing us to the most important things God wants us to know first. Genesis 1 told us that God is supreme, and that He created all things. And that all the natural world can only reproduce "after its kind". Then in Genesis 2 we were taught about obedience and what it means to sin. In this fourth chapter, we're introduced to one of the most common stumbling blocks of our human nature: jealousy, which leads to hatred, which, if left unchallenged, leads to murder. It is the same pattern that is highlighted in the New Testament:

> But every man is tempted, when he is drawn away of his own lust, and enticed. **Then when lust hath conceived, it bringeth forth sin: and sin, when it is finished, bringeth forth death.** (Jas 1:14-15)

The fault of Cain was not to have envious thoughts — that's what we all suffer with — but it was that he didn't do anything to dispel them. Notice that God, knowing the immaturity of His creation, steps in to teach Cain the right way to go about dealing with these exceptionally strong feelings:

> And the LORD said unto Cain, Why art thou wroth? and why is thy countenance fallen? If thou doest well, shalt thou not be accepted? and if thou doest not well, sin lieth at the door. And unto thee shall be his desire, and thou shalt rule over him. (Gen 4:6-7)

Notice that what God is describing is a process whereby Cain might learn to master his own natural feelings.

1) Acknowledge the feelings. Name them for what they are. Acknowledge the truth that these feelings have taken hold.

> Why art thou wroth? and why is thy countenance fallen?

2) Remind yourself that there is a way out, and that the end result *will* be better if you take action now.

> If thou doest well, shalt thou not be accepted?

3) Think about the consequences of allowing sin to take hold on your feelings. These feelings will eventually lead to actions.

> if thou doest not well, sin lieth at the door

4) Admit that the natural state of mankind is for sin to desire to surface. Our hearts and minds are naturally susceptible and will willingly go along with it.

> unto thee shall be [sin's] desire

5) So action is needed now to stop it in its tracks. Your will is strong enough to rule over sin while it is yet in its infancy your mind.

> *thou shalt rule over him*

This is the pattern, provided by God Himself, at the very start of His book, this book He gave us as a manual for the human mind and body. In the chapter we go on to see how Cain ignored that advice and instead gave free reign to his envy, which led to hatred, and this hatred led to a terrible consequence.

God is telling us that it's always too late when we're in the field with a stone in our hand. Murder, theft, adultery, whatever it is, has to be stopped in its infancy while we are yet strong enough to rule over it. This means we have to recognise when we have evil feelings, face up to our own human nature, remind ourselves of the blessings of right actions, and the consequences of inaction.

It was Cain's *inaction* that killed Abel.

Food for thought

v3-4 - Whilst there are differences between the sacrifices that Cain and Abel brought, we know that the reason why God respected one and not the other does not relate to the sacrifices but rather to the attitude of the ones making the sacrifices. Hebrews 11:4 says that the missing element in Cain was faith.

v19 - We can see echoes of this verse in Genesis 6:2.

Genesis 5

What is God's image and likeness?

If we look back at Genesis 1, we see that God made mankind in His own image:

> And God said, Let us make man in our image, after our likeness: and let them have dominion over the fish of the sea, and over the fowl of the air, and over the cattle, and over all the earth, and over every creeping thing that creepeth upon the earth. So God created man in his own image, in the image of God created he him; male and female created he them. (Gen 1:26-27)

Now that Adam has had a child, this child is in *his* image and likeness. The specific contrast between the two is being made here at the start of chapter 5:

> This is the book of the generations of Adam. In the day that God created man, **in the likeness of God made he him;** Male and female created he them; and blessed them, and called their name Adam, in the day when they were created. And Adam lived an hundred and thirty years, and **begat a son in his own likeness,**

***after* his *image*;** *and called his name Seth: (Gen 5:1-3)*

The point is being made that God made Adam in His image, and everyone who came after was in Adam's image.

There are two specific words used: "Image" and "Likeness".

Image: This word is used mostly of cast metal or carved images of idols that the people made. So it refers to the physical resemblance, for example:

> *Then ye shall drive out all the inhabitants of the land from before you, and destroy all their pictures, and destroy all their molten images, and quite pluck down all their high places: (Num 33:52)*

Likeness: This is used elsewhere in the Bible to mean something like, but not the same, as something else. For example:

> *Also out of the midst thereof came the likeness of four living creatures. And this was their appearance; they had the likeness of a man. (Eze 1:5)*

I suppose we're being told that everyone is individual, yet of the same form.

It's interesting that Cain is not described as being in Adam's likeness. Only Seth is. And then after this statement, there is this long list of descendants, leading up to Noah and his sons. I think what we're being told here is that this is the lineage that was faithful to God, where the likeness to Adam (the man made in the image and likeness of God) was passed down in their character and way of life.

Food for thought

v3-29 - This list of dying sons of Adam is actually the line through which Christ came. So, even so early in the Biblical record, the scene is being set for Adam's seed, the saviour (see Gen 3:15).

v24 - Enoch, who "walked with God" shows a way of behaving that pleased God – see Micah 6:8. Of course walking with God requires agreement with His laws:

Can two walk together, except they be agreed? (Amo 3:3)

Genesis 6

The eyes of the LORD

Verse 8 is short but incredibly important:

> *But Noah found grace in the eyes of the LORD. (Gen 6:8)*

It tells us that even though Noah wasn't perfect, there was something about his walk that caused God to want to save him. "Grace" means "undeserved favour". The next verse elaborates:

> *These are the generations of Noah: Noah was a just man and perfect in his generations, and Noah walked with God. (Gen 6:9)*

So Noah was just (morally perfect) and he walked with God. These phrases are what are picked up in the book of Micah:

> *He hath shewed thee, O man, what is good; and what doth the LORD require of thee, but to **do justly**, and to love mercy, and to **walk humbly with thy God**? (Mic 6:8)*

How had God shown the people of Israel at Micah's time what He required of them? Is it possible that He simply expected them to have read about Noah?

The point is this. If we want to find grace in the eyes of God, we have to be walking with Him as Noah and scores of others did. This phrase epitomises what separates God's people (the ones He wishes to save) and the wicked (the ones He wishes to judge). One group seeks a way back to God, since Adam and Eve initially walked with God in the garden of Eden and then lost that privilege:

> *And they heard the voice of the LORD God walking in the garden in the cool of the day: and Adam and his wife hid themselves from the presence of the LORD God amongst the trees of the garden. (Gen 3:8)*

The other group seeks to hide themselves from God's all seeing, all knowing gaze, shrinking away from His presence.

Ultimately this is futile, since God sees our manner of life, whether we are near to Him or far away, whether they are deeds of darkness or of light:

> *And **God saw** the light, that it was good: and God divided the light from the darkness. (Gen 1:4)*
>
> *And **GOD saw** that the wickedness of man was great in the earth, and that every imagination of the thoughts of his heart was only evil continually. ... But Noah found grace **in the eyes of the LORD**. (Gen 6:5, 8)*

Food for thought

v2 - That the sons of God "saw" the women were "fair" and so "took" them, echoes Eve's response to the fruit of the tree of life – Genesis 3:6. So Eve's behaviour is seen to be manifest in the sons born to Adam and his descendants.

v9 - We should not read lightly that Noah "walked with God". He was in a minority but was doing what Abraham would later be called to do (see Genesis 17:1) and what Jesus calls us to do (see Matthew 5:48).

v22 - Noah, the just man, did everything according to what God commanded him. We see the same commendation in Genesis 7:5 and 16. Is this something that could be said of us?

Genesis 7

How did all the animals fit on the Ark?

Some people think that it's impossible to get two of all animals onto a ship. Some go so far as to say the Bible is fiction because of it. When I hear this kind of accusation, I wonder whether they have ever walked aboard a cruise liner?

Consider the enormous size of the ark:

> And this is the fashion which thou shalt make it of: The length of the ark shall be three hundred cubits, the breadth of it fifty cubits, and the height of it thirty cubits. (Gen 6:15)

A cubit is about half a yard or metre, so this ship was about 150 metres long and 25m wide, which is the same length and width as an average size cruise liner today which could accommodate 1000 passengers plus crew.

Perhaps also they have not properly considered the animal kingdom. Think about all the large animals you know of. How many can you list? Once you've listed the Elephant, Rhinos, the great cats and the cattle, you're pretty much done with the big animals. Then there's the large reptiles, snakes and lizards, but not many of those are large species. If you imagine placing all of these next to each other, you have perhaps a school gym sized area.

Now imagine the animals that are the next size down: wolves, large birds, sheep, and so on. All of these take up much less room, and still there are not all that many species. Perhaps another school hall full. The place where there's an explosion in variety are in the small and tiny species, the birds and insect life, small rodents and lizards. Mathematically speaking though, while these are numerous, they do not take up much volume of space, so these might take only about as much space as the largest creatures.

So with multiple decks and the size of a cruise liner, we can easily conclude there was not only space to get the animals on, but also the necessary space for food stocks.

Food for thought

v6 - When Noah was six hundred years old we are only 1656 years after creation. This will help to give us some idea of a time frame in Genesis. Nor should we think of Noah and his family as primitive when we consider the making of the ark. Adam was the pinnacle of creation so what do we think was possible 1600 years later? Consider the advances that mankind has made in the last 1000 years!

v11 - The opening of the windows of heaven is used by the prophet in Isaiah 24:18 as a metaphor to speak of a later judgement.

Genesis 8

The evidence of the flood beneath our feet

Consider the brevity with which the book of Genesis covers the first few thousand years of mankind's history.

Now consider that two thirds of this entire chapter are devoted to describing the receding of the water. Doesn't that strike you as odd?

Here are some of the words used to describe the water:

- asswaged
- stopped
- restrained
- returned
- abated
- decreased continually
- dried up
- dry

Clearly there is intentionality with God describing this particular event in such detail. In other words, this is God saying "Look at this! It's important!"

The reason for this, to my mind, is that God is drawing attention to the vast amounts of water, and the enormous geological effect this was having on the world. When you consider how much silt was contained in that water, you can begin to imagine the effect of that gradual receding, gradual laying down of silt, and forming of the earth's surface that we see today.

Here in the UK where I'm writing from, there are in places hundreds of meters deep of this silt, which covers the entire land-mass apart from the mountain areas. I have seen borehole reports of shafts sunk 300m deep, where all the way down are seen the sedimentary layers created by this flood — and recorded in these reports are shells of sea creatures, and even still rotting vegetation. This clearly backs up the flood account.

So in this chapter God may be showing us the proof for the flood, which if we only look beneath our feet, we can still see clearly in the public record.

Food for thought

v15-16 - God had instructed Noah to enter the ark even though it was not raining (Genesis 7:1) And now, even though Noah knew that the ground was dry he waited for God to give him instructions to leave the ark.

v22 - God's promise that "day and night shall not cease" is used in Jeremiah 33:20 as a test that men can use, considering the existence of Israel as an evidence that God exists and keeps His word.

Genesis 9

Never again!

Notice that as Noah steps forth into a new creation, God gives over that creation totally to Noah and his descendants:

> And God blessed Noah and his sons, and said unto them, Be fruitful, and multiply, and replenish the earth. And the fear of you and the dread of you shall be upon every beast of the earth, and upon every fowl of the air, upon all that moveth upon the earth, and upon all the fishes of the sea; into your hand are they delivered. Every moving thing that liveth shall be meat for you; even as the green herb have I given you all things. (Gen 9:1-3)

This is the language of total dominion.

It is like this because Noah, the only one who was faithful, has overcome the sin that destroyed the rest of mankind, and has triumphed. His reward is to be given the world that God has taken away from man.

Yet there are some things still withheld from Noah. The power to take life from another man, and the power to drink blood. While God delivers the flesh of every beast into Noah's hands for food, God specifically omits the blood:

> *But flesh with the life thereof, which is the blood thereof, shall ye not eat. (Gen 9:4)*

And while God delivers the life of every beast into Noah's hands, God specifically omits mankind:

> *And surely your blood of your lives will I require; at the hand of every beast will I require it, and at the hand of man; at the hand of every man's brother will I require the life of man. Whoso sheddeth man's blood, by man shall his blood be shed: for in the image of God made he man. (Gen 9:5-6)*

Do you think God is specifically is referring to Caan and Abel here?:

> *And Cain talked with Abel his brother: and it came to pass, when they were in the field, that Cain rose up against Abel his brother, and slew him. And the LORD said unto Cain, Where is Abel thy brother? And he said, I know not: Am I my brother's keeper? And he said, What hast thou done?* **the voice of thy brother's blood crieth unto me from the ground.** *(Gen 4:8-10)*

God appears to be saying that the start of man's wickedness was at that act of Cain's, and that this mentality of violence and murder spread to all of mankind:

> *And God said unto Noah, The end of all flesh is come before me; for the earth is filled with violence through them; and, behold, I will destroy them with the earth. (Gen 6:13)*

This blood-letting had to stop, and God ended it by ending their lives in a bloodless death — drowning. Now that He was starting again, He would do so with new rules and penalties surrounding the shedding of blood, so that never again would the whole earth end up going in the way of Cain.

What God is effectively doing, is bringing the consequences of murder within the lifetime of the murderer. By saying He will require the blood of a murdered man at the hand of their murderer, whether man or beast, He is saying that they will not get away with it in their own lifetime.

This means that since the time of Noah, God has been actively managing mankind, by punishing those who spill blood. He does this primarily by ensuring that He sets up rulers who will punish such actions:

> Let every soul be subject unto the higher powers. For there is no power but of God: the powers that be are ordained of God. ... For he is the minister of God to thee for good. But if thou do that which is evil, be afraid; for he beareth not the sword in vain: for he is the minister of God, a revenger to execute wrath upon him that doeth evil. (Rom 13:1, 4)

This new order, instituted after the flood, would mean that never again would God need to intervene on a global scale to destroy mankind. And this is how, with confidence, God could promise:

> And God spake unto Noah, and to his sons with him, saying, And I, behold, I establish my covenant with you, and with your seed after you; And with every living creature that is with you, of the fowl, of the cattle, and of every beast of the earth with you; from all that go out of the ark, to every beast of the earth. And I will

establish my covenant with you; neither shall all flesh be cut off any more by the waters of a flood; neither shall there any more be a flood to destroy the earth. (Gen 9:8-11)

Food for thought

Verse 1 - The flood marked a new beginning – it was like a new creation – hence the commandment echoes the commandment given to Adam (Gen 1:28)

Verse 11 - In saying that He will no more destroy the earth with a flood, it demonstrates that the flood was universal. Since this time there have been regular local floods which cause destruction throughout history, but never again a worldwide flood.

Genesis 10

Noah's Grandsons

We've all heard of Shem, Ham and Japheth, but how about the sons of Japheth?

> *Now these are the generations of the sons of Noah, Shem, Ham, and Japheth: and unto them were sons born after the flood. The sons of Japheth; Gomer, and Magog, and Madai, and Javan, and Tubal, and Meshech, and Tiras. And the sons of Gomer; Ashkenaz, and Riphath, and Togarmah. And the sons of Javan; Elishah, and Tarshish, Kittim, and Dodanim. By these were the isles of the Gentiles divided in their lands; every one after his tongue, after their families, in their nations.* (Gen 10:1-5)

We're told here that the lands of the gentiles were populated from these people. That means that, probably, you and I were descended from them.

You may find it interesting to note that several of these names appear again in a prophecy of the last days. How many of those names can you find in Ezekiel 38? What could the meaning of this be?

Food for thought

Verse 9 - Nimrod's qualities as a "hunter" are nothing to be proud of. Hunting is not one of the skills that specifically God endorses. In fact Esau, the hunter, is contrasted unfavourably with Jacob – Gen 25:27 .

Verse 11 - That a flood will never cover the earth to destroy it is a feature drawn on by the Psalmist – Psa 104:9 – when the Psalmist says that God has set bounds to prevent a flood.

Verses 1,6,15,19 - the city of Sidon (means "fishery") was named after the great grandson of Noah; Sidon still exists under the name of Saida and has various archaeological sites authenticating the Bible as an accurate historical record going back to Genesis. Sidon/Saida is 20 miles north of Tyre in Lebanon.

Genesis 11

Be fruitful, and multiply, and replenish the earth

Here in Genesis 11 God has to act to forcibly spread people over the face of the earth:

> *So the LORD scattered them abroad from thence upon the face of all the earth: and they left off to build the city. (Gen 11:8)*

Why?

The answer is found in His earlier words of commandment to Adam. In fact, it is the only thing He commanded Adam to do apart from not eating of the tree of knowledge:

> *And God blessed them, and God said unto them, Be fruitful, and multiply, and replenish the earth, and subdue it: and have dominion over the fish of the sea, and over the fowl of the air, and over every living thing that moveth upon the earth. (Gen 1:28)*

Implicit in this commission is that they needed to cover the earth, because there would be no other way of replenishing the earth, or of having dominion over every living thing.

So right from the start of the creation we can see that it was God's plan to fill the world with people.

The same commandment is given to Noah after the flood, given that he and his family are now the new Adam, so to speak:

> *And God blessed Noah and his sons, and said unto them, Be fruitful, and multiply, and replenish the earth. (Gen 9:1)*

and again in verse 7, if there is any doubt as to the importance:

> *And you, be ye fruitful, and multiply; bring forth abundantly in the earth, and multiply therein. (Gen 9:7)*

With that in mind, we can now understand how disappointed God was when His people chose instead to go directly against His request, disobeying Him:

> *And they said, Go to, let us build us a city and a tower, whose top may reach unto heaven; and let us make us a name, **lest we be scattered abroad upon the face of the whole earth**. (Gen 11:4)*

In the face of this disobedience, God sent the angel to confound their languages, finally achieving what He had always intended them to do.

> *So the LORD **scattered them abroad from thence upon the face of all the earth**: and they left off to build the city. Therefore is the name of it called Babel; because the LORD did there confound the language of all the earth: and from thence did the LORD **scatter them abroad upon the face of all the earth**. (Gen 11:8-9)*

Food for thought

Verse 10 - Genesis 10 has given us the table of nations — all the sons of Noah's children. Now we return to Shem because it is through the seed of Shem that the promises are going to be fulfilled.

Verse 30 - Consider how many barren women eventually bore significant sons. This is a foreshadowing of the way that God would be the father of Messiah.

Genesis 12

Babel, the promises, and you

> *And I will bless them that bless thee, and curse him that curseth thee: and in thee shall all families of the earth be blessed. (Gen 12:3)*

Consider this. This account of God's promise to Abram is the first event recorded after the disastrous incident of the tower of Babel. These vitally important promises (for they impact all people, all nations, and all scripture that comes after this point) are therefore given in the context of Babel. How so?

The angel had come down and seen what the people of the world were up to. He saw that they had organised themselves for the purposes of coming together as one, in one location:

> *And they said, Go to, let us build us a city and a tower, whose top may reach unto heaven; and let us make us a name, **lest we be scattered abroad upon the face of the whole earth.** (Gen 11:4)*

It is their sole purpose to avoid this "scattering upon the face of the whole earth", and it is this that the angel notices and specifically deals with:

> Go to, let us go down, and there confound their language, that they may not understand one another's speech. So **the LORD scattered them abroad from thence upon the face of all the earth**: and they left off to build the city. Therefore is the name of it called Babel; because the LORD did there confound the language of all the earth: and from thence did the LORD **scatter them abroad upon the face of all the earth**. (Gen 11:7-9)

Why should this have been such a problem? It is because on the first page of the Bible, in the creation account, it is this that is stated as the purpose for mankind:

> And God blessed them, and God said unto them, **Be fruitful, and multiply, and replenish the earth**, and subdue it: and have dominion over the fish of the sea, and over the fowl of the air, and over every living thing that moveth upon the earth. (Gen 1:28)

And the very first and only recorded commandment God gave to Noah when he stepped off the ark is:

> Go forth of the ark, thou, and thy wife, and thy sons, and thy sons' wives with thee. Bring forth with thee every living thing that is with thee, of all flesh, both of fowl, and of cattle, and of every creeping thing that creepeth upon the earth; that they may breed abundantly in the earth, and **be fruitful, and multiply upon the earth**. (Gen 8:16-17)

This is repeated again and again, so that the importance could not be missed:

> *And God blessed Noah and his sons, and said unto them,* **Be fruitful, and multiply, and replenish the earth.** *... And you, be ye fruitful, and multiply; bring forth abundantly in the earth, and multiply therein.* (Gen 9:1, 7)

So with this context, can you see why it was evil to specifically do the opposite, in direct opposition to the commandment God had given?

> *And they said, Go to, let us build us a city and a tower...* **lest we be scattered abroad upon the face of the whole earth.** *(Gen 11:4)*

At this point we are introduced to Terah, Abram's father, who is the first person, after the flood, to be recorded as doing what God had commanded:

> *And Terah took Abram his son, and Lot the son of Haran his son's son, and Sarai his daughter in law, his son Abram's wife; and they went forth with them from Ur of the Chaldees, to go into the land of Canaan; and they came unto Haran, and dwelt there.* (Gen 11:31)

This action of obedience is rewarded in chapter 12 with God's promise to Abram. It is by looking at the promise in this correct historical context that we can see the following:

- God is reinforcing the commandment "get out of your country"
- God tells Abram that if he keeps the commandment God will help him enact it: "I will make you a great nation"
- God is emphasising that keeping the commandment brings blessings and benefits: "I will bless you"

- He is acknowledging that in all the earth, Abram is the only one keeping the commandment, so that it is vital for Abram to succeed so that others would follow his example: "in you all the families of the earth shall be blessed"

So in essence, God's wonderful promises to Abram are as a result of obedience. Obedience is what God requires of us, no matter who we are or what age we live in. It is the same throughout the Bible, from Abraham, to Jesus, and to us:

> And in thy seed shall all the nations of the earth be blessed; **because thou hast obeyed my voice.** (Gen 22:18)
>
> For as by [Adam]'s disobedience many were made sinners, so **by the obedience of [Jesus] shall many be made righteous.** (Rom 5:19)
>
> Know ye not, that to whom ye yield yourselves servants to **obey**, his servants ye are to whom ye **obey**; whether of sin unto death, or of **obedience** unto righteousness? But God be thanked, that ye were the servants of sin, but ye have **obeyed from the heart** that form of doctrine which was delivered you. Being then made free from sin, ye became the servants of righteousness. (Rom 6:16-18)

If we are to be servants of righteousness, as Abraham was, and to benefit from these promises, it is a simple matter of obedience to God's word. The alternative, either by commission or omission, is to be part of Babel.

Food for thought

Verses 1-4 - The call of Abram was 2024 years after creation - 443 years after the end of the flood

Verse 2 - The promise of being a "great nation" was to be fulfilled through Israel, not through natural strength, but because of their adoption of God's laws and commandments, which in turn made them blessed by God and "great" in the eyes of other nations. See Deut 4:6-8.

Verse 10 - That Abram went to "sojourn" in Egypt shows that he viewed the excursion into Egypt as a temporary event.

Genesis 13

Bible questions

And he went on his journeys from the south even to Bethel, unto the place where his tent had been at the beginning, between Bethel and Hai; (Gen 13:3)

Question 1) Abraham travelled all the way back to where he started from. There he called on the Lord:

Unto the place of the altar, which he had made there at the first: and there Abram called on the name of the LORD. (Gen 13:4)

Why did he make this journey, and why did he call on the LORD in this particular place? Can you find scripture to explain it?

Question 2) Abraham and Lot, and their wives, are major Bible characters. Can you explain why Abraham's wife is mentioned here, but not Lot's wife? Does the Bible even tell us what Lot's wife was called?

And Abram went up out of Egypt, he, and his wife, and all that he had, and Lot with him, into the south. (Gen 13:1)

Food for thought

Verse 8 - Abram's words to Lot, "For we be brethren," should mark the way that we respond to our brethren in issues of preference. The cessation of strife between brethren is far more important than personal "rights". After all, Abram was the one to whom the land was promised, and yet he gave Lot the first choice as to which part he wanted.

Verse 12 - Lot pitched his tent "towards Sodom," so initially he was outside the city, but apparently facing it. Very soon he was dwelling "in Sodom" (Gen 14:12). Then sitting "in the gate" where the elders sat (Gen 19:1). Thus we see how, once on a downward road, it is so easy to progress to a potentially destructive position. The direction we are facing is so important in setting the direction of travel in our lives (Heb 12:2, Rom 8:1).

Genesis 14

Led by God, or led by … ?

Here is a truly fascinating chapter, and one that isn't spoken of as often as the other chapters in Genesis we've covered so far. However, it has some very important learning points. Have you noticed what the key thread of the chapters is? The clue is in Abraham's snub to the King of Sodom at the end:

> *And Abram said to the king of Sodom, I have lift up mine hand unto the LORD, the most high God, the possessor of heaven and earth, That I will not take from a thread even to a shoelatchet, and that I will not take any thing that is thine, lest thou shouldest say, I have made Abram rich: (Gen 14:22-23)*

The King had offered all the spoil to Abraham, a considerable fortune, yet Abraham refused it. Why?

Well, Abraham's herdsmen had had a quarrel with Lot's herdsmen. It seems that they had become so wealthy and numerous that they were rather on top of one another:

> *And Lot also, which went with Abram, had flocks, and herds, and*

tents. And the land was not able to bear them, that they might dwell together: for their substance was great, so that they could not dwell together. And there was a strife between the herdmen of Abram's cattle and the herdmen of Lot's cattle: and the Canaanite and the Perizzite dwelled then in the land. (Gen 13:5-7)

Notice, however, the additional detail: "and the Canaanite and the Perizzite dwelled then in the land."

The land could not bear them, but the land was also host to the Canaanites and Perizzites. Why is that detail inserted there? It is because of the earlier prophecy by Noah concerning the Canaanites:

And he said, Cursed be Canaan; a servant of servants shall he be unto his brethren. And he said, Blessed be the LORD God of Shem; and Canaan shall be his servant. (Gen 9:25-26)

Abraham and Lot were Shemites, and the reason for their crowded conditions was not specifically that they were rich, it was that the Canaanites were in the land. Don't forget here that God had promised the land of the Canaanites to Abraham and his descendants:

And Abram took Sarai his wife, and Lot his brother's son, and all their substance that they had gathered, and the souls that they had gotten in Haran; and they went forth to go into the land of Canaan; and into the land of Canaan they came... And the LORD appeared unto Abram, and said, Unto thy seed will I give this land: and there builded he an altar unto the LORD, who appeared unto him. (Gen 12:5-7)

Abraham was therefore to understand that the prophecy made by Noah, that Canaan would be the servant, was to be fulfilled in his family line, and by their occupation and ownership of the Canaanite's land. In other words, because of what happened at the time of Noah, Canaan was to be stripped of his land and it was to be given to Abraham.

Jesus reinforces this principle in his parable of the talents, where the one talent of the sinning party is given to the righteous party:

> *His lord answered and said unto him, Thou wicked and slothful servant... Take therefore the talent from him, and give it unto him which hath ten talents. For unto every one that hath shall be given, and he shall have abundance: but from him that hath not shall be taken away even that which he hath. (Mat 25:26-29)*

This principle is played out again and again in the life of Abraham, where wealth is taken from the wicked and given to the just. Take for example his time in Egypt, or in Philistine country, or his battle in this chapter. Take also for example Isaac's dwelling with the Philistines, and Jacob's dwelling in Haran. Each time the riches pass from the wicked to the just, by God's intervention:

> *Then Isaac sowed in that land, and received in the same year an hundredfold: and the LORD blessed him. And the man waxed great, and went forward, and grew until he became very great: For he had possession of flocks, and possession of herds, and great store of servants: and the Philistines envied him ... And Abimelech said unto Isaac, Go from us; for thou art much mightier than we. (Gen 26:12-16)*

So what does this tell us of Lot? It tells us that as long as Lot was with Abraham, in Abraham's camp, he was blessed with Abraham. But as soon as he moved away and looked to the perceived riches of the wicked, he decreased. It is because by making this move, he had instead allied himself with those whom were prophecied to be Abraham's servants. Lot is the man who was in the family of the faithful and left it to join the wicked.

Based on the pattern we have looked at, it is no wonder that in this chapter we find all of Lot's riches going to Abraham:

And he brought back all the goods, and also brought again his brother Lot, and his goods, and the women also, and the people. (Gen 14:16)

As spoils of war, the King of Sodom rightfully acknowledges that these are now all in Abraham's ownership. This man at least is wise and humble enough to recognise his own position. Lot on the other hand, who the Bible says is a righteous man, made the fatal mistake of not taking this second chance that he had been given to rejoin the family of the faithful. Instead, we find him once again reunited with his goods, and back in the city of Sodom:

And there came two angels to Sodom at even; and Lot sat in the gate of Sodom. (Gen 19:1)

But there is a twist in the story. There is a hidden reason why Lot made these unwise choices, whilst being a righteous man. There is a hidden lesson that shows us what our duty in life is to do, if we are not to suffer the fate of Lot.

There is one person that influenced Lot to do what he did, to leave Abraham, to pitch his tent towards Sodom, to enter the city, and to sit in the gate. She was someone who loved the city life, the riches, and the glory of being the wife of one who had high office in the land. She was the one who persuaded Lot to return to Sodom when Abraham had saved him, and the one who made him linger when the angels came to get them out of that evil place. How do we know this? Because she was the one who, finally rid of those goods which had become such a shackle to them, turned back and longed to have them again.

> *Remember Lot's wife. (Luk 17:32)*

Lot's demise is easy to be explained, and simple to avoid. He, like Abraham, was a righteous man, yet unlike Abraham, failed to keep the first commandment that God had given to man in regard to his wife:

> *Unto the woman he said, I will greatly multiply thy sorrow and thy conception; in sorrow thou shalt bring forth children; and thy desire shall be to thy husband, and* **he shall rule over thee.** *(Gen 3:16)*

It is in the words of Jesus to remember Lot's wife, and in the words of Genesis that show her looking back and turning into a pillar of salt, that we see her character. We learn that it was she who was the one thread in Lot's life that explains each of his missteps, and his ultimate downfall. It was by listening to this woman, and not having the strength to overrule her, that his weakness lay.

Do we (men) have this weakness to be led when we should lead? Do we (women) have this weakness to dominate when we should submit? It is a simple point, yet so hard to do. Yet our salvation and that of our families may well depend on it. Sarah showed the right way when she called Abraham her Lord, and by going with him wherever he went. She allowed Abraham to set the tone and the direction, which in turn allowed Abraham to listen carefully to the LORD and go where he had been asked to go. The choice before us today is stark. We make the choice of whether to be in Abraham's camp, heir to the promises, or Lot's camp, in with the unrighteous, in the way we operate our relationships: Sarah and salvation, or Lot's wife and ruination.

Food for thought

Verse 14 - That Abraham had 318 trained servants born in his house indicates something of the size of Abraham's camp. These servants would have wives and children, and in addition there may have been servants that were not born in his house - an indication as to why Lot had to separate from him - but why, then, was Abraham fearful of Pharaoh? (Genesis 12:12)

Verse 19, 22 - Both Melchisedec and Abram recognised the status of God – "possessor of heaven and earth". That appreciation determined how those two individuals would respond to circumstances around them. Do we, appreciating that all creation belongs to God, behave appropriately?

Genesis 15

Abram: The father of salvation by faith

Reading the first few verses of chapter 15 it is clear Abram needs some reassurance about God's promises.

After these things the word of the LORD came unto Abram in a vision, saying, Fear not, Abram: I am thy shield, and thy exceeding great reward. And Abram said, Lord GOD, what wilt thou give me, seeing I go childless, and the steward of my house is this Eliezer of Damascus? And Abram said, Behold, to me thou hast given no seed: and, lo, one born in my house is mine heir. (Gen 15:1-3)

This should give us encouragement, because Abraham is the prime example of faith given in the Old Testament, and so, if he needed help, then we should be encouraged to ask for it too. The important thing is that, after the reassurance, Abraham did believe God, and so we have one of the most important verses in scripture recorded for us:

And he believed in the LORD; and He counted it to him for righteousness. (Gen 15:6)

This verse is the corner stone of salvation. It is quoted in Hebrews:

> *For if Abraham were justified by works, he hath whereof to glory; but not before God. For what saith the scripture? Abraham believed God, and it was counted unto him for righteousness. (Rom 4:2-3)*

And upon this is built the doctrine of justification (being made perfect) by faith:

> *But now the righteousness of God without the law is manifested, being witnessed by the law and the prophets; Even the righteousness of God which is by faith of Jesus Christ unto all and upon all them that believe: for there is no difference: For all have sinned, and come short of the glory of God; Being justified freely by his grace through the redemption that is in Christ Jesus ... that he might be just, and the justifier of him which believeth in Jesus. (Rom 3:21-26)*

Abram's Amorite Allies

Abram had been promised the land, yet it was currently too big for him to take possession of it. He had just fought with several inhabitants of the land and prevailed, but he had done this with the aid of his neighbours, the Amorites (see Genesis 14:13,24).

Having allies was all well and good, but he could see a time ahead where his faithful adherence to God would bring him into conflict with them too. Hence his question to God in this chapter:

> *And he said, Lord GOD, whereby shall I know that I shall inherit it? (Gen 15:8)*

In other words: 'If I'm to inherit the land, something needs to happen to displace my Amorite allies. I can't fight them because I'm friends with them and I need them.' God answers this by giving Abraham a vision where He allays his concerns about his Amorite allies. They would be conquered by Abraham's descendants, after the Exodus:

> *And when the sun was going down, a deep sleep fell upon Abram; and, lo, an horror of great darkness fell upon him. And he said unto Abram, Know of a surety that thy seed shall be a stranger in a land that is not theirs, and shall serve them; and they shall afflict them four hundred years; And also that nation, whom they shall serve, will I judge: and afterward shall they come out with great substance. And thou shalt go to thy fathers in peace; thou shalt be buried in a good old age. But* **in the fourth generation they shall come hither again: for the iniquity of the Amorites is not yet full.** *(Gen 15:12-16)*

Food for thought

Verse 1 - "I am thy shield and … reward" is God's response to Abraham's unwillingness to be made rich by the king of Sodom.

Verse 6 - The apostle Paul tells us in Romans 4:23 that the promise was written down for Abraham as well as for us.

Whilst Abraham is described as being counted righteous by faith, he is not the first man describes as righteous. We have, for example Noah (Gen 7:1). Of course the basis for Noah's righteousness was the same as for Abraham – he believed what God had told him.

Genesis 16

Abram hearkened to the voice of Sarai

Sarah was tired of waiting for a child, and decided to take matters into her own hands:

> Now Sarai Abram's wife bare him no children: and she had an handmaid, an Egyptian, whose name was Hagar. And Sarai said unto Abram, Behold now, the LORD hath restrained me from bearing: I pray thee, go in unto my maid; it may be that I may obtain children by her. And Abram hearkened to the voice of Sarai. (Gen 16:1-2)

The wording here about Abraham's involvement is specific:

> And Abram hearkened to the voice of Sarai.

We're only a few chapters in to the start of the Bible. Are there any echoes from previous chapters that you notice here?

There was another couple at the start of Genesis who had similar problems with who listened to whom:

And unto Adam he said, **Because thou hast hearkened unto the voice of thy wife***, and hast eaten of the tree, of which I commanded thee, saying, Thou shalt not eat of it: cursed is the ground for thy sake; in sorrow shalt thou eat of it all the days of thy life; (Gen 3:17)*

Notice how specific God is in His wording:

Because thou hast hearkened unto the voice of thy wife.

It is the act of listening to Eve that God calls out as wrong. Remember that it was Eve who was deceived, and not Adam. Adam's problem wasn't that he was deceived. No, he went along with it knowing that it was wrong. Adam's problem was that he let his wife's words overrule him.

God's solution to the problem of husbands being naturally inclined to allow their judgement to be overruled by their heart — their desire for their wife — is addressed there and then by God, and He puts a "fix" in place:

Unto the woman he said, I will greatly multiply thy sorrow and thy conception; in sorrow thou shalt bring forth children; and thy desire shall be to thy husband, and **he shall rule over thee***. (Gen 3:16)*

This pronouncement "he shall rule over thee" is there to stop such things happening again. It is there as a statement by God that within a marriage, the man is to have the power to overrule the wife when it comes to important decisions.

This is shown worked out in a practical example in the law of Moses, where there is the facility for the husband to overrule his wife if she has vowed something rash:

> *And if she had at all an husband, when she vowed, or uttered ought out of her lips, wherewith she bound her soul; And her husband heard it, and held his peace at her in the day that he heard it: then her vows shall stand, and her bonds wherewith she bound her soul shall stand. But if her husband disallowed her on the day that he heard it; then he shall make her vow which she vowed, and that which she uttered with her lips, wherewith she bound her soul, of none effect: and the LORD shall forgive her. (Num 30:6-8)*

Here clearly the pronouncement of Genesis 3 is upheld. This clearly is the way Adam ought to have behaved when he saw Eve reach for the fruit. This clearly is the way Abraham should have behaved when Sarai came to him with that outlandish proposal.

Sarai understood this, and this is why she is entirely justified when she blames Abraham for allowing it:

> *And Sarai said unto Abram, My wrong be upon thee: I have given my maid into thy bosom; and when she saw that she had conceived, I was despised in her eyes: the LORD judge between me and thee. (Gen 16:5)*

And thus Abraham was berated.

In today's culture it is harder than ever to take God's pronouncement seriously. If Abraham and Sarah could barely manage it in their day, what hope do we have? Furthermore, we may well, in our marital relationship, have gone so far down the wrong path that reversing course seems impossible. But as always, God provides a way, and has in fact built it into the very nature of man and woman since that day in the garden. Man he has made more physically strong. It has been established by scientific studies that the male's upper body strength is between two to four times that of women, and that's an astonishing difference. The man's voice is generally an octave lower. In height he is 14cm taller on average. These differences, all stacked in favour of men, appear to be God's way of ensuring that the men have a head start in keeping the order which He established in the beginning of Genesis. It is only when culture denies or denigrates these differences that we have real trouble, and it is up to each of us to avoid the influence of this Godless culture as much as possible.

Both Abraham and Sarah learned from this situation, so that later, she called him her lord, re-establishing an ideal that is picked up in the new testament as a lesson for all of us:

> *For after this manner in the old time the holy women also, who trusted in God, adorned themselves, being in subjection unto their own husbands: Even as Sara obeyed Abraham, calling him lord: whose daughters ye are, as long as ye do well, and are not afraid with any amazement. (1Pe 3:5-6)*

Food for thought

Verse 11-12 - God allowed Abraham and Sarah to fulfil their own plans for the promise to be fulfilled. However their plans were to prove disastrous. Ishmael was to be a "wild man" (Gen 16:12). How often do we try to rush God's purpose, only to find that what we have done brings us problems?

Verse 16 - So we have a clear time marker. Abraham was 75 when he left Haran (Gen 12:5). He is now 86 when Ishmael was born - 11 years after he left Haran.

Genesis 17

Abraham's Circumcision Implementation Committee (ACIC)

I n this issue of the ACIC newsletter we decided to tell you, our members, a little about our founder, and how he came to set up the ACIC, 100 years ago.

Abraham first heard about circumcision from God, who told him that it would be a sign of the covenant between them:

> *And I will establish my covenant between me and thee and thy seed after thee in their generations for an everlasting covenant, to be a God unto thee, and to thy seed after thee ... This is my covenant, which ye shall keep, between me and you and thy seed after thee; Every man child among you shall be circumcised. (Gen 17:7, 10)*

Immediately he gathered together the leading men of his household and told them about it. They talked about circumcision, the importance of it, and what it entailed. They decided they needed to know more about the procedure, so they quickly set up a committee to plan the circumcision implementation, which was a large task given the size of

Abraham's household.

A month later the committee met for the first time, bringing with them their preliminary thoughts. Each man presented his findings and they were discussed. It was decided that circumcision of all the males in one go was a large and complex task, and ought to be done in stages. Several of the committee were given the task to set up a working group whose remit it would be to canvas opinion and work out a realistic schedule.

Two month later (the next meeting fell on a holiday so it was postponed) it was reported that the working group was now set up. Queries were raised by one committee member about the possibility of infection, and as this worried the committee a great deal, they decided to find and consult a medical expert. Questions were also raised about the negative impression mass circumcision would give to the neighbouring families. This was tabled for discussion at the next meeting.

A few meetings later, 6 months after God contacted Abraham, the working group presented a devastating report. Everyone they had asked about circumcision was dead set against it. The objections ranged from medical concerns with the procedure, concerns over seeing blood, loss of working time, permanent scarring, ridicule in the village, and the list went on. It was at this stage that a permanent committee was set up to address each concern and take the project forward.

Today, on our centennial year, while as yet no circumcision has been carried out ...

[end of fictional excerpt from the ACIC newsletter]

That was a fictional attempt at putting the situation into the context of our modern times, and I'm sure it's not a million miles from how it could have gone with Abraham too, had he delayed. Notice, in contrast, how Abraham actually did it:

> *And Abraham took Ishmael his son, and all that were born in his house, and all that were bought with his money, every male among the men of Abraham's house; and circumcised the flesh of their foreskin **in the selfsame day**, as God had said unto him. And Abraham was ninety years old and nine, when he was circumcised in the flesh of his foreskin. And Ishmael his son was thirteen years old, when he was circumcised in the flesh of his foreskin. **In the selfsame day** was Abraham circumcised, and Ishmael his son. And all the men of his house, born in the house, and bought with money of the stranger, were circumcised with him. (Gen 17:23-27)*

It's quite a contrast to how we might have gone about it. And he was a 99 year old man! Do we sometimes talk rather than do what God has asked us to do? If we leave something difficult for just one day, that one day inevitably turns into weeks and months. What God asked us to do might never get done.

In contrast, see Moses and Zipporah who had allowed delay to turn into (perhaps) years, until finally God sent an angel to punish Moses for his inaction:

> *And it came to pass by the way in the inn, that the LORD met him, and sought to kill him. Then Zipporah took a sharp stone, and cut off the foreskin of her son, and cast it at his feet, and said, Surely a bloody husband art thou to me. So he let him go: then she said, A bloody husband thou art, because of the circumcision. (Exo 4:24-26)*

It highlights to us the very real concerns one might have with the procedure. Evidently Zipporah had been resisting it, and Moses had been unable to persuade her. For Abraham to have, in one day, been able to command his entire household to carry this out, shows us that he was truly the ruler over his own house, after the pattern God established in the garden of Eden:

> *Unto the woman he said, I will greatly multiply thy sorrow and thy conception; in sorrow thou shalt bring forth children; and thy desire shall be to thy husband, and he shall rule over thee. (Gen 3:16)*

> *One that ruleth well his own house, having his children in subjection with all gravity; (For if a man know not how to rule his own house, how shall he take care of the church of God?) (1Ti 3:4-5)*

Food for thought

Verse 1 - Another mark of the passage of time. At age 99, we are now 24 years on from when Abraham left Haran - and he receives the covenant of circumcision.

Verse 17 - Abraham, like Zacharias many years later, saw his age as a barrier to fathering a child. However, he believed the "impossible" whereas Zacharias doubted the same promise (see Luke 1:18-20).

Genesis 18

Abraham and Lot: The Godly and worldly household

In the previous chapter Abram has had his name changed to Abraham, and having been re-born as this new man (so to speak), he has entered into a covenant with God:

> *This is my covenant, which ye shall keep, between me and you and thy seed after thee; Every man child among you shall be circumcised. (Gen 17:10)*

The next event is after the chapter break, so we don't usually connect the two. However, it is continuing the narrative from chapter 17 in one piece without a break:

> *In the selfsame day was Abraham circumcised, and Ishmael his son. And all the men of his house, born in the house, and bought with money of the stranger, were circumcised with him. And the LORD appeared unto him in the plains of Mamre: and he sat in the tent door in the heat of the day. (Gen 17:26 - 18:1)*

So we are led to conclude here that the arrival of the three angels is as a consequence of Abraham and his household being taken into covenant relationship with God.

The specific thing that we are given to focus on, is that Abraham had managed to command his entire household to be circumcised in a single day. That speaks volumes about Abraham's ability to teach his offspring about God.

But think about this for a moment. Who else used to be a part of that household, and would have been circumcised along with it? It was Lot and his family. These left Abraham and pitched their tent towards Sodom, and now they are dwelling in that city. The contrast between Abraham and his tent, and Lot and his city house, couldn't be more stark.

The text gives us several more subtle comparisons between the two men and the way they had led their families:

> *And he lift up his eyes and looked, and, lo, three men stood by him: and when he saw them, he ran to meet them from the tent door, and bowed himself toward the ground, ... For I know him, that* **he will command his children and his household after him, and they shall keep the way of the LORD**, *to do justice and judgment; that the LORD may bring upon Abraham that which he hath spoken of him.* (Gen 18:2, 19)

Abraham had come away from the region where the city and tower of Babel were set up. He now dwelled in a tent to show that he was a stranger and pilgrim in the earth. His wife obediently stayed in the tent as he went to meet strangers. He commands his household and children to keep the way of the LORD. Notice in this phrase that God is specifically referencing the event of the circumcision of his whole household:

> *And Abraham took Ishmael his son, and all that were born in his house, and all that were bought with his money, every male among the men of Abraham's house; and circumcised the flesh of their foreskin in the selfsame day, as God had said unto him.* (Gen 17:23)

In other words, Abraham had commanded them, and they did it.

Compare this with Lot, who had gone back to city life, dwelling in a house to show that he was settled in that wicked city. His wife turned back rather than obeying a specific instruction not to look back. His family laughed at him; quite the opposite of being under his authority:

> *...Lot sat in the gate of Sodom: and Lot seeing them rose up to meet them; and he bowed himself with his face toward the ground; And he said, Behold now, my lords, turn in, I pray you, into your servant's house, and tarry all night, and wash your feet, and ye shall rise up early, and go on your ways ... And Lot went out, and spake unto his sons in law, which married his daughters, and said, Up, get you out of this place; for the LORD will destroy this city. But he seemed as one that mocked unto his sons in law. ... But his wife looked back from behind him, and she became a pillar of salt.* (Gen 19:1-2, 14, 26)

There are lessons here more numerable than it is possible to mention. For us, do we accept the word of the LORD and do it, or do we regress towards a life of doing the will of the world around us? Perhaps more pertinent for many of us, do we command our households to serve the LORD, or do they barely know where we stand?

Food for thought

Verse 2 - The "three men" are actually angels. Two of them go off to Sodom (Gen 19:1) whilst "the LORD" stays with Abraham (Gen 18:13). We may never know when we are entertaining angels, but our Father certainly uses them today (Heb 13:2).

Verse 12 - In laughing and calling Abram "Lord" in her heart, Sarah was demonstrating that her respect for her husband was not simply an outward show. It was a way of life. This attitude is presented as a pattern for believing women today - 1 Peter 3:6.

Genesis 19

Comparing Lot with Abraham

We could talk all day about what happened in this chapter. It is the most stark and sobering warning to us all about the nature of God and the way He expects men and women to behave in the world He created. The destruction of Sodom and Gomorrah is now the second judgment we read about in Genesis, with the first being the flood. Given the non-linear way populations increase, it's quite possible that as many people died in this judgment as died in the flood.

In order to learn from this terrible event, the chapter asks us to look at it jointly through the eyes of Lot and Abraham. We know this because in v28-29 the viewpoint of the account moves from Lot to Abraham, and we then see it through his eyes:

> And **he looked** toward Sodom and Gomorrah, and toward all the land of the plain, **and beheld**, and, lo, the smoke of the country went up as the smoke of a furnace. (Gen 19:28)

In fact, we learn in the next verse that Lot was saved *because* of Abraham:

And it came to pass, when God destroyed the cities of the plain, that God remembered Abraham, and sent Lot out of the midst of the overthrow, when he overthrew the cities in the which Lot dwelt. (Gen 19:29)

The main lesson seems to be, that at the final judgment of this wicked world, we can either be part of it, or looking on from afar.

Some contrasting examples

So let's look at some of the contrasts between the two men, living at the same time, who had the same knowledge of God and the same opportunity to serve Him. These are not criticisms of Lot, but a way of looking at two righteous men, one who was wise and stayed separate from godless society, and the other who was foolish enough to dwell in the midst of it.

	Abraham		Lot	
Obedience	Genesis 22:2-3	Did what God asked him immediately, in faith	Genesis 19:15-19	Delayed doing what he had been asked. Argued.
Family	Genesis 17:23-27	Had his household under his authority. They did what he asked immediately.	Genesis 19:14	His example had no effect on his in-laws. They refused to do as he asked.
Resisting evil	Genesis 14:14-16	Had built up defences to resist the evil people around him.	Genesis 19:9	Had given up all military protection in return for the "safety" of a city.

Food for thought

Verse 9 - From the record it would appear that Lot went to Sodom and became a judge in the city as he was sitting in the gate (v1) - the place of judgment - (see for example, Ruth 4:1,10-11). In this position he "vexed his righteous soul" (2 Peter 2:8). From this we learn that the servant of God has no place trying to solve the world's ills.

Verse 13 - The utter destruction of the wicked is shown by Abraham seeing smoke rising as a furnace. This idea is echoed (Rev 19:3) when salvation is come to the earth. Salvation cannot come to the earth in its fullness whilst wickedness is still present.

Genesis 20

Why did Abraham move?

> And Abraham journeyed from thence toward the south country, and dwelled between Kadesh and Shur, and sojourned in Gerar. (Gen 20:1)

Why did Abraham move away? He had a good thing going where he was, with plenty of servants and livestock. He was in league with his neighbours too. So why upset all that? And why move into Philistine country?

The answer is given later, in a description given at the time of Isaac, his son:

> And there was a famine in the land, beside the first famine that was in the days of Abraham. And Isaac went unto Abimelech king of the Philistines unto Gerar. (Gen 26:1)

Here we are told of an earlier famine in the time of Abraham. The implication is that since Isaac went to Gerar because of famine, that this is why Abraham went there the first time too. The land of Gerar is on the plain of the Philistines which is well watered compared with the mountainous regions of Hebron where Abraham had been living. How do we know this is the case? Today in Israel an aquifer is known to exist called the "coastal aquifer", stretching along the coast from Gaza past Tel Aviv. It is here that Abraham escaped to. As a sojourner with no fixed abode, it was easier for Abraham and his family to move to better pastures for a while.

Notice that while the plain of Sodom had been a well watered area, and much nearer, but it was no longer so after the destruction of Sodom:

> *And Lot lifted up his eyes, and beheld all the plain of Jordan, that it was well watered every where,* **before the LORD destroyed Sodom and Gomorrah**, *even as the garden of the LORD, like the land of Egypt, as thou comest unto Zoar. (Gen 13:10)*

Food for thought

Verse 4 - Abimelech clearly had an understanding of the laws of God. We should not presume that when Abraham was in the land of Canaan that he and his group were the only ones who feared the Lord. Clearly Abimelech did, and we have already come across Melchisedec in Genesis 14. Abraham left a Godless place and moved to the land of Canaan where, even though there were wicked people, there were some faithful individuals.

Verse 7 - We are told here that Abraham was a prophet, which explains Psalm 105:13-15, that God actually spoke to Abimelech and reproved him.

Genesis 21

Who do we listen to?

This chapter is about who we listen to. Abraham had been too hasty in listening to the words of his wife:

> *And Sarai said unto Abram, Behold now, the LORD hath restrained me from bearing: I pray thee, go in unto my maid; it may be that I may obtain children by her.* **And Abram hearkened to the voice of Sarai.** *(Gen 16:2)*

And that had put him in this difficult situation where he had a child with his wife's servant. The proverbs say this about the situation:

> *For three things the earth is disquieted, and for four which it cannot bear: For a servant when he reigneth; and a fool when he is filled with meat; For an odious woman when she is married; and an handmaid that is heir to her mistress. (Pro 30:21-23)*

A handmaid that succeeds her mistress is something unbearable, says the proverb, and such was the situation with Hagar and Sarah:

> *And he went in unto Hagar, and she conceived: and when she saw that she had conceived, her mistress was despised in her eyes. And Sarai said unto Abram, My wrong be upon thee: I have given my maid into thy bosom; and when she saw that she had conceived, I was despised in her eyes: the LORD judge between me and thee. (Gen 16:4-5)*

Sarah recognises that her husband should not have listened to her on that occasion. The implication is that he knew better, but gave in.

Abraham seems to have learned from this, and in our chapter we find him having to deal with the aftermath. This time, even though Sarah's words have a ring of wisdom about them, he isn't going to grant her wish:

> *And Sarah saw the son of Hagar the Egyptian, which she had born unto Abraham, mocking. Wherefore she said unto Abraham, Cast out this bondwoman and her son: for the son of this bondwoman shall not be heir with my son, even with Isaac. And the thing was very grievous in Abraham's sight because of his son. (Gen 21:9-11)*

Yet, curiously, on this occasion God Himself steps in and tells Abraham to listen to his wife:

> *And God said unto Abraham, Let it not be grievous in thy sight because of the lad, and because of thy bondwoman; in all that Sarah hath said unto thee, hearken unto her voice; for in Isaac shall thy seed be called. (Gen 21:12)*

Clearly Sarah is the wiser here, and the one who remembers the words of God's promise correctly (see Gen 17:19). The new testament picks up on these words and reveals something extraordinary we might not have otherwise seen:

> *But as then he that was born after the flesh persecuted him that was born after the Spirit, even so it is now. Nevertheless what saith the scripture? Cast out the bondwoman and her son: for the son of the bondwoman shall not be heir with the son of the freewoman.* (Gal 4:29-30)

Galatians tells us that Ishmael persecuted Isaac. Clearly there was more to it than mocking. And in this the wisdom of Sarah is revealed. Did she have in mind the jealousy of Cain, the firstborn of Adam and Eve, who when he was succeeded by his younger brother, killed him? Is it possible that this is where things were going and that Sarah could see it?

After the servant and the boy (now 14 years old) were cast out, the scripture tells us that Hagar wept and cried out. Yet the record is clear that God does not hear her. Instead, He hears the cries of the boy:

> *she said, Let me not see the death of the child. And she sat over against him, and lift up her voice, and wept. And* **God heard the voice of the lad***; and the angel of God called to Hagar out of heaven, and said unto her, What aileth thee, Hagar? fear not; for* **God hath heard the voice of the lad** *where he is.* (Gen 21:16-17)

God did not hear the voice of the handmaid who had despised Sarah, of whom the promised seed was born. He did hear the boy, who had been born to Abraham, and had been circumcised in his household as a sign of being in covenant with God through Abraham. Thus Abraham's blessing passed to the boy, who himself obtained promises, and God was with him to make him a great nation:

And also of the son of the bondwoman will I make a nation, because he is thy seed ... And God was with the lad; and he grew, and dwelt in the wilderness, and became an archer. (Gen 21:13, 20)

Food for thought

Verse 2 - We might think it quite normal to say "Sarah conceived and bare Abraham a son"; however Abraham was already a father to Ishmael. The emphasis on naming both parents is to stress that Isaac is the very child of promise spoken of in Genesis 18:10.

Verse 23 - The wary words of Abimelech and Phicol, that Abraham would not "deal falsely" with them, may indicate that they knew about his escapade when he passed off his wife as his sister when he was in Kadesh. From this we learn that our indiscretions done in one place can affect the way that others think of us who were not directly involved in the initial indiscretion.

Genesis 22

The place I will show you

Why did God ask Abraham to go to a specific place to carry out this sacrifice?

> *And he said, Take now thy son, thine only son Isaac, whom thou lovest, and get thee into the land of Moriah; and offer him there for a burnt offering upon one of the mountains which I will tell thee of. (Gen 22:2)*

Could Abraham not have demonstrated his faith in God anywhere? Notice in the wording of the verses; God would show him a specific mountain in the place called Moriah. So Abraham takes a journey to Moriah, but while he is still a long way away, he leaves his servants behind:

> *Then on the third day Abraham lifted up his eyes, and saw the place afar off. And Abraham said unto his young men, Abide ye here with the ass; and I and the lad will go yonder and worship, and come again to you. (Gen 22:4-5)*

Again, why? We assume it was because he needed to be alone with his son, which I'm sure is part of the answer, but could it also be that he didn't want to reveal the place that God was to show him? Again, in v9 the wording specifically emphasises the place:

And they came to the place which God had told him of... (Gen 22:9)

Abraham recognises the special significance of the place God has shown him, because after he has demonstrated his faith, and God provides a sacrifice of a ram instead of Isaac; he gives the place a name:

And Abraham called the name of that place Jehovahjireh: as it is said to this day, In the mount of the LORD it shall be seen. (Gen 22:14)

He now returns to his men, and returns home. No-one is any the wiser about what occurred, and no-one knows about the place except Abraham and Isaac.

Come with me forward in time several hundreds of years. Fourteen generations have passed, and all knowledge of the place is a dim memory. The story of Abraham and Isaac has been written down in scripture for any Israelite to read, and the story is handed down from generation to generation, but the location of the place is never revealed. But now we come to David, and a time in his life where his sin has caused great wrath from God upon his people Israel. The angel of death has been sent out and is ravaging the land with plague. David wants desperately to plead with God and offer sacrifices at the tabernacle, but is too afraid of the angel to get to it (1Ch 21:29-30). With nothing else to do, and in desperation, David throws himself down before God and confesses his sin. God answers him with the name of a place...

> *Then the angel of the LORD commanded Gad to say to David, that David should go up, and set up an altar unto the LORD in the threshingfloor of Ornan the Jebusite. (1Ch 21:18)*

Why should there be an altar there, in that place? Perhaps there is something special about the place?

David knew. God answered his prayer from heaven (v26) and sanctified the altar:

> *And David built there an altar unto the LORD, and offered burnt offerings and peace offerings, and called upon the LORD; and he answered him from heaven by fire upon the altar of burnt offering. (1Ch 21:26)*

David remembered the story of Moriah, and the place revealed to Abraham but now lost in the mists of time. He remembered a specific detail from Genesis 22:9

> *And they came to the place which God had told him of;* **and Abraham built an altar there.**

Then David said:

> *This is the house of the Lord God, and* **this is the altar of the burnt offering for Israel.** *And David commanded... to build the house of God. (1 Ch 22:1)*

Food for thought

Verse 2 - When Abraham took Isaac to Mount Moriah to offer him as a burnt sacrifice do we think that Abraham had any thoughts about Melchisedec whom he had met in that area (Genesis 14) some years earlier?

Verse 4 - We know that Jesus rose on the third day "according to the Scriptures" (see 1Cor 15:3-4). Have you considered what Scriptures Paul had in mind? Maybe this is one of them. At the end of a three day journey Isaac is sacrificed and raised from the dead, figuratively speaking.

Genesis 23

The parable of Abraham's field

> *And the field of Ephron, which was in Machpelah, which was before Mamre, the field, and the cave which was therein, and all the trees that were in the field, that were in all the borders round about, were made sure Unto Abraham for a possession in the presence of the children of Heth, before all that went in at the gate of his city. And after this, Abraham buried Sarah his wife in the cave of the field of Machpelah before Mamre: the same is Hebron in the land of Canaan. And the field, and the cave that is therein, were made sure unto Abraham for a possession of a buryingplace by the sons of Heth. (Gen 23:17-20)*

Notice in the Genesis record of this transaction, how many times the "field" is mentioned. It's a curious detail, because all Abraham needed was the cave at the end of the field:

> *And he communed with them, saying ... intreat for me to Ephron the son of Zohar, That he may give me the cave of Machpelah, which he hath, which is in the end of his field; for as much money as it is worth he shall give it me for a possession of a buryingplace*

amongst you. (Gen 23:8-9)

So Abraham ended up buying a field so that he could have the thing that was worth a lot to him, namely the burial cave for his wife.

It cost Abraham a lot of money:

And Abraham hearkened unto Ephron; and Abraham weighed to Ephron the silver, which he had named in the audience of the sons of Heth, four hundred shekels of silver, current money with the merchant. (Gen 23:16)

The field became Abraham's possession, so that many years after the promise to inherit the land, he now had a legal claim to at least some of it. Jesus tells a parable of a man buying a field, and there are many similarities between that parable and this event:

Again, the kingdom of heaven is like unto treasure hid in a field; the which when a man hath found, he hideth, and for joy thereof goeth and selleth all that he hath, and buyeth that field. (Mat 13:44)

I wonder if Jesus is think of this event? Was Sarah, Abraham's wife, his greatest treasure? Was Abraham using "all that he had" to buy the field, namely a stake in the promised land?

The book of Proverbs seems to make that link too, in describing the virtuous wife as a man's greatest treasure:

Who can find a virtuous woman? for her price is far above rubies. The heart of her husband doth safely trust in her, so that he shall have no need of spoil. She will do him good and not evil all the days of her life. (Pro 31:10-12)

It would seem apt that this proverb and Jesus's parable were based on Sarah, as a testament to her lifelong dedication to Abraham.

Food for thought

Verse 4 - In describing himself as "a stranger and a sojourner" Abraham demonstrated that he expected the promises to be fulfilled at a later date - by implication when he is raised from the dead. This sets the pattern for our life. We should live in this world as "strangers and pilgrims" (1 Peter 2:11), and as such, should not follow the behaviour of those amongst whom we live.

Verse 12-13 - In insisting in paying for the land in which he buried Sarah we see that Abraham lay no claim on the land which he had been promised.

Verse 15-16 - Whilst Abraham paid 400 shekels of silver for a piece of land to bury Sarah, David paid Araunah 50 shekels of silver for the threshing floor and the animals in 2Samuel 24:24, and Jeremiah buys a field for 17 shekels of silver in Jeremiah 32:9. We can conclude that the price that Abraham paid was possibly way above the market value of the piece of land he bought. But he did not complain. This is the attitude of a sojourner in a foreign land. He accepts the customs of the land if they do not violate the principles of God.

Genesis 24

Isaac's long wait

> *And I will make thee swear by the LORD, the God of heaven, and the God of the earth, that thou shalt not take a wife unto my son of the daughters of the Canaanites, among whom I dwell: (Gen 24:3)*

It was of utmost importance to Abraham that his son not marry a Canaanite. These people, descended from Ham, had been cursed by Noah after Ham's sin:

> *And Noah awoke from his wine, and knew what his younger son had done unto him. And he said, Cursed be Canaan; a servant of servants shall he be unto his brethren. And he said, Blessed be the LORD God of Shem; and Canaan shall be his servant. (Gen 9:24-26)*

Abraham had respect to the words of this curse, and so it would have been inappropriate to marry into Canaan's line. Further to this, it was Canaan's offspring who inhabited Sodom and Gomorrah, a testament to their tendency to evil:

*And Canaan begat Sidon his firstborn, and **Heth** ... and afterward were the families of the Canaanites spread abroad. And the border of the Canaanites was from Sidon, as thou comest to Gerar, unto Gaza; as thou goest, unto Sodom, and Gomorrah, and Admah, and Zeboim, even unto Lasha. (Gen 10:15-19)*

We know also that a generation later, Isaac's own son ignored his grandfather's wishes and took, not one, but two Canaanite wives. The comment is that these women were so wicked, they were a source of great distress to his father and mother:

And Esau was forty years old when he took to wife Judith the daughter of Beeri the Hittite, and Bashemath the daughter of Elon the Hittite: (Gen 26:34)

*And Rebekah said to Isaac, I am weary of my life because of the **daughters of Heth**: if Jacob take a wife of the daughters of Heth, such as these which are of the daughters of the land, what good shall my life do me? (Gen 27:46)*

Notice that they are specifically called "daughters of Heth", the son of Canaan.

Abraham, then, had a choice. Either his son marries a Canaanite in contravention of God's will, or he stays single. It seems for a long while Isaac did stay single, since he was forty years old when he married Rebekah. The long wait was an enormous test of Isaac's faith, for he knew that the promise was of his offspring becoming a great nation. He knew that, since God keeps His promises, there would be a faithful woman for him, if he were only to wait for God's provision. That provision came in the form of Rebekah — not the daughter of Canaan — but of the same faithful line as Abraham:

> *And it came to pass after these things, that it was told Abraham, saying, Behold, Milcah, she hath also born children unto thy brother Nahor; ... And Bethuel begat Rebekah: these eight Milcah did bear to Nahor, Abraham's brother. (Gen 22:20, 23)*

This is how Abraham knew when to send his servant to find a wife for his son, and presumably why Abraham waited until his son was forty years old. He was waiting for Rebekah to be of marriageable age.

Food for thought

Verse 18-20 - The record is wishing to stress that Rebekah was enthusiastic to meet the needs of Abraham's servant. Notice that twice she "hasted" and once we are told that she "ran". Those words are unnecessary in describing her actions unless we are expected to see her commitments to service. This characteristic she shared with Abraham (Gen 18:7).

Verse 27 - That the servant knew Abraham's God was a god of "mercy and truth" shows us that God does not change. When God revealed himself to Moses using these same words (Exo 34:6) He was showing Moses aspects of His character which had always been there.

Genesis 25

Esau the profane person

By Esau's words he is confessing that he does not believe in the resurrection:

> And Esau said, Behold, I am at the point to die: and what profit shall this birthright do to me? (Gen 25:32)

In contrast, Abraham, Isaac and Jacob all did:

> By faith he sojourned in the land of promise, as in a strange country, dwelling in tabernacles with Isaac and Jacob, the heirs with him of the same promise: ... These all died in faith, not having received the promises, but having seen them afar off, and were persuaded of them, and embraced them, and confessed that they were strangers and pilgrims on the earth. (Heb 11:9, 13)

Hebrews makes a specific point about Esau in the next chapter. Having commended his brother, father and grandfather for their faith in the promises, it says this about Esau:

Lest there be any fornicator, or profane person, as Esau, who for one morsel of meat sold his birthright. For ye know how that afterward, when he would have inherited the blessing, he was rejected: for he found no place of repentance, though he sought it carefully with tears. (Heb 12:16-17)

The point is made that to obtain the promises takes endurance, something that Esau spectacularly failed to show. In contrast, it was shown to the uttermost by Jesus:

For consider him that endured such contradiction of sinners against himself, **lest ye be wearied and faint***in your minds. Ye have not yet resisted unto blood, striving against sin. (Heb 12:3-4)*

The contrast is stark. Jesus resisted his impulses even to the death, and yet Esau was unable even to overcome his temporary hunger — for one morsel of meat sold his birthright. See the similar wording that links the two passages together:

And Esau said to Jacob, Feed me, I pray thee, with that same red pottage; for ***I am faint****: therefore was his name called Edom. And Jacob said, Sell me this day thy birthright. And Esau said, Behold,* ***I am at the point to die****: and what profit shall this birthright do to me? (Gen 25:30-32)*

Jesus resisted his impulses for food for forty days, and then literally did die in order to inherit the promises to Abraham. Esau had the promise to Abraham in his hand, yet gave it away for one morsel.

Then Jacob gave Esau bread and pottage of lentiles; and he did eat and drink, and rose up, and went his way: thus Esau despised his birthright. (Gen 25:34)

The lesson that Hebrews draws from this, is that we should carefully prepare so that we do not fall short of the grace of God that secures our salvation.

Food for thought

Verse 1 - Keturah is here described as Abraham's wife, though in 1Chron 1:32 she is described as his concubine. As the record here is talking about after Sarah's death, does this indicate that Keturah's status changed from Concubine to wife at this time, and that she had been his concubine for some time before the death of Sarah?

Verse 7 - Another time marker. Abraham left Haran when he was 75 and died when he was 175 - so we are 100 years on from that time.

Genesis 26

Isaac's bodyguard

There is a pattern for Isaac's life that mimics the life of Abraham. For example, they each have to move from the promised land because of famine and live in Philistine or Egyptian country. Our lives will be uncertain like this too. We shouldn't assume we will always live in one place, as circumstances might change. Yet God will look after us wherever He sends us, just as He did with Abraham and Isaac and their families. Notice how God works with the simple fact that Rebekah is beautiful, to provide complete protection for Isaac and his family until they are strong enough to defend themselves:

> *And Isaac dwelt in Gerar: And the men of the place asked him of his wife; and he said, She is my sister: for he feared to say, She is my wife; lest, said he, the men of the place should kill me for Rebekah; because she was fair to look upon… And Abimelech charged all his people, saying, He that toucheth this man or his wife shall surely be put to death. (Gen 26:6-11)*

Notice how this passage precedes Isaac's prosperity in the land, using the phrase "Then Isaac sowed in the land…" by which we conclude that this protection was part of God's blessing that made all the difference:

> Then Isaac sowed in that land, and received in the same year an hundredfold: and the LORD blessed him. And the man waxed great, and went forward, and grew until he became very great: (Gen 26:12-13)

We should be content to live amongst other people, other nations, and other religions, like Abraham and Isaac. Our attitude must be neighbourly and respectful, like theirs. And when God provides people who might look after us, for whatever their own motive might be, we should accept it graciously, because it may have been arranged by God.

Food for thought

Verse 18 - Isaac, in digging wells and not fighting for them when the inhabitants of the land took them, demonstrates that he had the "mind of Christ" (Phl 2:5), who taught us to "turn the other cheek", and "when he was reviled, reviled not again" but trusted in the LORD to deliver him (1 Pet 2:23).

Verse 26-27 - Maybe Isaac's confidence was a consequence of the fact that God had told him to "fear not" (Gen 26:24).

Genesis 27

He found no place of repentance

> *And when Esau heard the words of his father, he cried with a great and exceeding bitter cry, and said unto his father, Bless me, even me also, O my father. ... And Esau said unto his father, Hast thou but one blessing, my father? bless me, even me also, O my father. And Esau lifted up his voice, and wept. (Gen 27:34, 38)*

Esau comes in to the presence of his father Isaac expecting to be given the blessing of the firstborn, and in one moment this is taken away and replaced with the realisation that he had lost it to his brother. Notice the "exceeding bitter cry" and weeping which Genesis makes a point in recording for us. The new testament book of Hebrews comments on this incident and says:

> *For ye know how that afterward, when he would have inherited the blessing, he was rejected: for he found no place of repentance, though he sought it carefully with tears. (Heb 12:17)*

The commentary suggests that this is a cameo of the judgement, where some will come expecting a reward, and instead, find they have been rejected.

Isaac, even though he realised the deception that Jacob had perpetrated, wouldn't accept Esau's tears. Did Isaac recognise God's hand in taking the blessing away from his eldest son? Maybe he was even relieved that the right conclusion had been reached? We know that Isaac already knew this in his heart, because earlier we read that both Isaac and Rebekah were grieved at the Canaanite wives Esau had chosen. In fact, this is the context in which this very incident is introduced:

> *And Esau was forty years old when he took to wife Judith the daughter of Beeri the Hittite, and Bashemath the daughter of Elon the Hittite: Which were a grief of mind unto Isaac and to Rebekah ... And it came to pass, that when Isaac was old, and his eyes were dim, so that he could not see, he called Esau his eldest son, and said unto him, My son: and he said unto him, Behold, here am I. (Gen 26:34-35, 27:1)*

Not only had Esau not paid attention to his father and mother, he had also not paid attention to Abraham his grandfather, who specifically had this to say about the people of the land:

> *And I will make thee swear by the LORD, the God of heaven, and the God of the earth, that thou shalt not take a wife unto my son of the daughters of the Canaanites, among whom I dwell: (Gen 24:3)*

How could the promises of God to Abraham pass into Canaanite lineage, when it was God's plan to destroy the Canaanites to inherit their land generations later? Due to his ill considered marriages, Esau had made it impossible for him to inherit the promises. Here is what the scripture tells us later that God said about these people:

> *But of the cities of these people, which the LORD thy God doth give thee for an inheritance, thou shalt save alive nothing that breatheth: But thou shalt utterly destroy them; namely, the Hittites, and the Amorites, the Canaanites, and the Perizzites, the Hivites, and the Jebusites; as the LORD thy God hath commanded thee: That they teach you not to do after all their abominations, which they have done unto their gods; so should ye sin against the LORD your God. (Deu 20:16-18)*

This careless attitude is also mentioned in Hebrews 12, where it calls Esau a "profane person" for despising his birthright and for his choice of women. The way he sold his birthright was careless, just like his attitude to his father's teaching, or God's teaching. To be careless was to despise it:

> *Wherefore lift up the hands which hang down, and the feeble knees; And make straight paths for your feet, lest that which is lame be turned out of the way; but let it rather be healed. Follow peace with all men, and holiness, without which no man shall see the Lord:* **Looking diligently lest any man fail of the grace of God;** *lest any root of bitterness springing up trouble you, and thereby many be defiled; Lest there be any fornicator, or profane person, as Esau, who for one morsel of meat sold his birthright. (Heb 12:12-16)*

For us there is still time to act to become diligent — the opposite of careless. The lesson is that we should prepare straight paths for ourselves, to take the time we have left to lift up what is limp and strengthen what is feeble. Esau took no time — was not prepared — for the day of judgement. And then, suddenly, it was too late.

Food for thought

Verse 1, 6 - Notice the tension. Esau was "his" son whereas Jacob was "her" son.

Verse 33 - We could conclude that Isaac "trembled very exceedingly" because he realised that if it had not been for the deception, he would have gone against what he knew was God's will, because of the comment made by God in Genesis 25:33 to Rebekah.

Genesis 28

Does it matter whom we marry?

It's easy to think of these stories in Genesis as being about familiar Bible characters, and not see the underlying reason we are being told about them. If the lives of Abraham, Isaac and Jacob were recorded for general spiritual teaching and motivation, whole books could be filled about them quite easily - but this is not what we see. We see concise specific detail, because God wishes to make specific and vitally important points for us to listen to. With that in mind let's look at the specific point being made in Chapter 28. Notice what is going on as we pick up the story:

> *And God Almighty bless thee, and make thee fruitful, and multiply thee, that thou mayest be a multitude of people; And give thee the blessing of Abraham, to thee, and to thy seed with thee; that thou mayest inherit the land wherein thou art a stranger, which God gave unto Abraham. (Gen 28:3-4)*

Isaac is here blessing Jacob a second time, after Jacob tricked Isaac into giving him the first blessing, and this time he is specifically handing over the Promises that God gave to Abraham. The wording is interesting and shows where Isaac's concerns lie:

- make thee fruitful
- multiply thee
- a multitude of people
- to thy seed with thee

That's four times in one sentence that Isaac mentions Jacob's descendants — but Jacob isn't married and doesn't have children! We can see that Isaac's mind is fully focused on passing the promises on, not just to one, but many generations after. So why did he say this to Jacob who had no wife? Why had he not passed these promises on to Esau, who *did* have wives and may have been well on the way to having a large family of his own? Esau wondered the same thing:

> *When Esau saw that Isaac had blessed Jacob, and sent him away to Padanaram, to take him a wife from thence; and that as he blessed him he gave him a charge, saying, Thou shalt not take a wife of the daughters of Canaan; And that Jacob obeyed his father and his mother, and was gone to Padanaram; (Gen 28:6-7)*

The implication of these verses are that Esau had *not* obeyed his father, and that he *had* taken wives from the daughters of Canaan:

> *And Esau seeing that the daughters of Canaan pleased not Isaac his father; Then went Esau unto Ishmael, and took unto the wives which he had Mahalath the daughter of Ishmael Abraham's son, the sister of Nebajoth, to be his wife. (Gen 28:8-9)*

The very reason Rebekah gives for sending Jacob away, is because of Esau's wives:

And Rebekah said to Isaac, I am weary of my life because of the daughters of Heth: if Jacob take a wife of the daughters of Heth, such as these which are of the daughters of the land, what good shall my life do me? (Gen 27:46)

Clearly the "daughters of the land" were not suitable to be the mothers of those who would inherit the promises. The challenge facing Isaac and Rebekah was to find a wife for Jacob who would not be contaminated with the abominable idolatry of the Canaanites, and had been brought up at least to be open to learning the truth about God. Hence we begin the chapter with Isaac's strongly worded commission:

And Isaac called Jacob, and blessed him, and charged him, and said unto him, Thou shalt not take a wife of the daughters of Canaan. Arise, go to Padanaram, to the house of Bethuel thy mother's father; and take thee a wife from thence of the daughters of Laban thy mother's brother. (Gen 28:1-2)

We can see the main point being specifically made by the chapter. It is that those who inherit the promises can not enter into marriage with those who do not have the potential to share that same focus on those promises. Esau demonstrated the attitude of one who didn't care about this, but Jacob "obeyed". As a result we find God visiting Jacob and confirming those promises to him personally, and not only that, but by particular emphasis on his descendants:

And thy seed shall be as the dust of the earth, and thou shalt spread abroad to the west, and to the east, and to the north, and to the south: and in thee and in thy seed shall all the families of the earth be blessed. (Gen 28:14)

The sole focus of these chapters is on marriage, and how to choose the right partner. Do you think sometimes we allow ourselves to be tricked into thinking the Bible is about more "spiritual" or ethereal things than the practical realities of life? Have we personally made a Bible study of what God thinks of marriage so that we can be sure to follow Jacob's example and avoid Esau's? Perhaps we're already married so we don't feel this is any longer relevant to us — but in that case, take a look at Isaac and Rebekah and see how relevant it was to them. Rebekah's life was being made a misery by the Godless attitude of her daughters in-law. Do you think maybe Isaac and Rebekah wished they had been more forthright with Esau about whom he should marry?

Food for thought

Verse 1 - The way in which Esau's hatred for Jacob was used to obtain a wife for Jacob was a mixture of deceit and expediency. Whilst it was clear that a wife from the inhabitants of the land was not good for Jacob, the hasty way the plan was conceived contrasted markedly with Abraham and Sarah's concern about finding a wife for Isaac (Gen 24:3-6). There was no ulterior motive with Abraham, which contrasts with that of Isaac and Rebekah. As time rolls on their plan turns out to give Jacob real problems. We should be careful always to ensure that we plan ahead so that we can do things in the correct way for the right reasons.

Verse 11 - The setting sun marks the beginning of Jacob's twenty year period away from the land of promise. He acquired a wife, two actually, and two concubines and eleven sons and great wealth. The section ends in Gen 32:31 when we see a sunrise. During this time Jacob learnt that he had to wait and trust that God would work out His plan, at His speed, using His methods.

Genesis 29

Finding a wife at the well

If you have been reading Genesis so far, you may have noticed that this is a repeat of what happened with Isaac and Rebekah. Even the commission given by the father to go and find the wife is the same. But there are important differences, and this is why this is presented to us. Because just as we seen in Abraham and Isaac the right way of doing things, we see in Isaac and Jacob the wrong way:

> *And I will make thee swear by the LORD, the God of heaven, and the God of the earth, that thou shalt not take a wife unto my son of the daughters of the Canaanites, among whom I dwell: But thou shalt go unto my country, and to my kindred, and take a wife unto my son Isaac. (Gen 24:3-4)*

> *And Isaac called Jacob, and blessed him, and charged him, and said unto him, Thou shalt not take a wife of the daughters of Canaan. Arise, go to Padanaram, to the house of Bethuel thy mother's father; and take thee a wife from thence of the daughters of Laban thy mother's brother. (Gen 28:1-2)*

The motivation in each case is good — to take a wife from a Godly family, not the idolatrous Canaanites. But the difference is immediately apparent when we look at how open Abraham leaves his request, to how specific Isaac makes his. In other words, Abraham is trusting in God to take care of it, and Isaac appears to be trying to engineer the event himself. The same pattern is seen when we look at the event at the well:

> *And he made his camels to kneel down without the city by a well of water at the time of the evening, even the time that women go out to draw water. And he said, O LORD God of my master Abraham, I pray thee, send me good speed this day, and shew kindness unto my master Abraham. (Gen 24:11-12)*

> *And he looked, and behold a well in the field, and, lo, there were three flocks of sheep lying by it; for out of that well they watered the flocks: and a great stone was upon the well's mouth. ... And Jacob said unto them, My brethren, whence be ye? And they said, Of Haran are we. And he said unto them, Know ye Laban the son of Nahor? And they said, We know him. (Gen 29:2, 4-5)*

Abraham's servant, realising that this mission is entirely in God's hands, arrives at the well and meekly prays for God to help. Jacob arrives at the well and begins to engineer the situation himself. There is no mention of prayer at any point with Jacob during this event. Then when the woman comes forward with her flocks, the men's actions are two opposites:

> *And Jacob kissed Rachel, and lifted up his voice, and wept. (Gen 29:11)*

> *And the man wondering at her held his peace, to wit whether the LORD had made his journey prosperous or not. (Gen 24:21)*

Jacob is acting as if this is a foregone conclusion. The servant of Abraham waits. Jacob lifted up his voice and wept, whereas the servant bowed down and praised the LORD:

> *And the man bowed down his head, and worshipped the LORD. (Gen 24:26)*

So we can see that Jacob and Isaac were trying to repeat the success God had granted Abraham, yet using none of the faith, trust, prayer, and meekness that made it a success in the first place. Whilst their motives were sound, they forgot to include God.

In our own lives, we may have the right motives. But do we meekly present our requests to God in prayer and let Him handle it? Or do we forget to pray and assume life will turn out as we planned it? The record is silent as to whom God intended for Jacob. I suspect, however, it was not Rachel, but rather Leah. You see, the huge thing that Jacob missed was that he was supposed to be watching the woman to see whether she would willingly serve others and meekly seek their well-being. As the servant of Abraham waited patiently he saw how Rebekah took it upon herself to serve him — a stranger. Jacob reversed this and, instead, served her:

> *And she said, Drink, my lord: and she hasted, and let down her pitcher upon her hand, and gave him drink. And when she had done giving him drink, she said, I will draw water for thy camels also, until they have done drinking. And she hasted, and emptied her pitcher into the trough, and ran again unto the well to draw water, and drew for all his camels. (Gen 24:18-20)*

And it came to pass, when Jacob saw Rachel the daughter of Laban his mother's brother, and the sheep of Laban his mother's brother, that Jacob went near, and rolled the stone from the well's mouth, and watered the flock of Laban his mother's brother. (Gen 29:10)

Food for thought

Verse 29-30 - We have seen there was favouritism in Jacobs family. Now he manifests it towards his two wives. Just as it caused problems at home for him it will cause problems for him in his own family. Surely we should be learning from these lives.

Verse 22 - In promising to give a tenth, Jacob is emulating his grandfather Abraham who gave a tenth "of all he had" to Melchisedec (Gen 14:20). Both events pre-date the law of Moses but show that already the concept of paying tithes was in force. It was probably instituted by God to the faithful and formalised in the law of Moses.

Genesis 30

The rivalry of Rachel and Leah explained

Talk about a dysfunctional family! If we have read this chapter before, we may have got so caught up in the drama of the story that we miss some of the spiritual significance of it. It is unusual in any story, whether fictional or historical, to go into such detail about childbearing. Have you wondered what the reason for it is? Clearly the two sisters, Rachel and Leah, were competing among themselves to see who could bear the most children. Is that normal? If this was the usual sibling rivalry, could it not have manifested itself in other ways like who wore the best clothes, who worked hardest in the field, who weighed the most or least, who could run fastest or was the prettiest or any other trait?

If we put the chapter in context, we soon find out. Jacob has been sent away from his home to go and find a wife. His father (Isaac) sends him off with these words:

> *Arise, go to Padanaram, to the house of Bethuel thy mother's father; and take thee a wife from thence of the daughters of Laban thy mother's brother. (Gen 28:2)*

then gives him this blessing:

> And God Almighty **bless thee**, and make thee **fruitful**, and **multiply thee**, that thou mayest **be a multitude of people**; And give thee **the blessing of Abraham**, to thee, and **to thy seed** with thee; that thou mayest inherit the land wherein thou art a stranger, which God gave unto Abraham. (Gen 28:3-4)

Its a completely unique commission to give to a young man. I've put in bold text where the emphasis is on childbearing, raising up a people, being fruitful, and also the "blessing of Abraham", which is:

> Seeing that Abraham shall surely become a great and mighty nation, and all the nations of the earth shall be blessed in him? (Gen 18:18)

Notice the emphasis on the "seed" of Abraham throughout the promises God gave him:

> For all the land which thou seest, to thee will I give it, and to thy seed for ever. And I will make thy seed as the dust of the earth: so that if a man can number the dust of the earth, then shall thy seed also be numbered. (Gen 13:15-16)

So we have far from a normal situation. A man who has just been passed the promises of his Grandfather Abraham, which all relate to a "seed", which means descendants, and how that they will be very numerous and grow into a great nation. How shocking it would be, then, for Rachel to discover she was barren, and to find that Leah was in line to fulfill these promises for Jacob rather than her? So this gives a spiritual dimension to the rivalry of the two women and why it focused solely on childbearing. In a way, this rivalry showed the faith that the two women had in the promises made to Abraham, and their respect for Jacob who obviously had told them of the promises and talked about them often. It gives us a peek into the daily life of this family, and allows us to see the focus of that family on the word of God despite all the challenges of life.

Food for thought

Verse 3 - The English translation "have children" more correctly should be "be builded by", catching the desire of Rachel to have children to bring on the fulfillment of the promises through her.

Verse 23 - Rachel said "God hath taken away my reproach," words which Elizabeth spoke after she was promised a child (Luke 1:25)

Genesis 31

God doesn't forget His promises

> And the LORD said unto Jacob, Return unto the land of thy fathers, and to thy kindred; and I will be with thee. (Gen 31:3)

In that verse we see a reminder to Jacob of the promise God gave to him when he was fleeing home:

> And, behold, I am with thee, and will keep thee in all places whither thou goest, and will bring thee again into this land; for I will not leave thee, until I have done that which I have spoken to thee of. (Gen 28:15)

It shows that God had been with Jacob all along. Looking at the wording of the promise, we can see that God had intended to bring him back home again, so we can conclude that the events surrounding Jacob's exit from Padan Aram were guided by Him.

Not only had God been watching over Jacob:

> And he said, Lift up now thine eyes, and see, all the rams which leap upon the cattle are ringstraked, speckled, and grisled:

*for **I have seen all that Laban doeth unto thee**. (Gen 31:12)*

He had also been ensuring his well-being in fulfillment of His promise "I will keep thee":

> And said unto them, I see your father's countenance, that it is not toward me as before; but the God of my father hath been with me. ... And your father hath deceived me, and changed my wages ten times; but God suffered him not to hurt me. ... Thus God hath taken away the cattle of your father, and given them to me. ... For all the riches which God hath taken from our father, that is ours, and our children's: now then, whatsoever God hath said unto thee, do. (Gen 31:5, 7, 9, 16)

The countenance of Laban

> *And Jacob beheld the **countenance** of Laban, and, behold, it was not toward him as before. (Gen 31:2)*

There is an important word of warning in this chapter. If a boss who had been friendly towards you changes their countenance towards you, it is probably time to leave their employment. It signals that they may be scheming your downfall, as is the case with Laban.

> *And your father hath deceived me, and changed my wages ten times; but **God suffered him not to hurt me**. (Gen 31:7)*

Is it possible that this man was starting to think about killing his son in law? This a scriptural phrase we may remember from how Cain is described when he considers murdering his brother:

> But unto Cain and to his offering he had not respect. And Cain was very wroth, and his countenance fell. And the LORD said unto Cain, Why art thou wroth? and why is thy **countenance** fallen? (Gen 4:5-6)

Food for thought

Verse 2 - Laban's scheming against Jacob seems to be becoming less effective. From Laban's perspective the wonderful blessing of having Jacob care for his flock, seems now to have turned to be a blessing upon Jacob. So Laban sees Jacob as a liability now. Hence his attitude changes.

Verse 41 - Because we read the details of the life of Jacob in a few chapters we may easily forget the long time periods involved. The events in the house of Laban cover 20 years. How would we deal with 20 years of frustration?

Genesis 32

Jacob's struggle

Had Esau forgotten all about his previous pledge to kill Jacob? Or were some of the old wounds still raw? It's hard to tell what Esau meant to do with his 400 men. Did he mean to attack Jacob? Was he perhaps actually frightened of his brother, knowing that the blessings upon him meant he possibly had a large band of servants by now? Were the 400 men just for insurance? I think it's clear what Jacob thought this army was for:

> And the messengers returned to Jacob, saying, We came to thy brother Esau, and also he cometh to meet thee, and four hundred men with him. Then Jacob was greatly afraid and distressed. (Gen 32:6-7)

Was Jacob right to be afraid? I think so. The Proverbs testify of the power of a gift to pacify anger:

> A gift in secret pacifieth anger: and a reward in the bosom strong wrath. (Pro 21:14)

It seems likely that Jacob's gifts pacified Esau's "strong wrath", and that prior to that point, Esau had meant to slay his brother. Jacob prays the following prayer before sending further gifts, and it seems that the strategy that saved him was as an answer to that prayer:

> *Deliver me, I pray thee, from the hand of my brother, from the hand of Esau: for I fear him, lest he will come and smite me, and the mother with the children. (Gen 32:11)*

It seems that the effect of this extreme event is that Jacob recognises that God's promises could be relied on. In the following words he quotes the promises given to him and to Abraham and Isaac, and like them, puts his faith in God's singular ability to keep his promises:

> *And Jacob said, O God of my father Abraham, and God of my father Isaac, the LORD which saidst unto me, Return unto thy country, and to thy kindred, and I will deal well with thee: I am not worthy of the least of all the mercies, and of all the truth, which thou hast shewed unto thy servant; for with my staff I passed over this Jordan; and now I am become two bands ... And thou saidst, I will surely do thee good, and make thy seed as the sand of the sea, which cannot be numbered for multitude. (Gen 32:9-12)*

For us too, it is by faith in God's promises that we are saved, it is not by our own works. It is the gift of God.

> *For by grace are ye saved through faith; and that not of yourselves: it is the gift of God: (Eph 2:8)*

Food for thought

Verse 28 - The idea of being a prince and having power with God is used by the prophet (Hos 12:3) to remind Israel of the high position that they had fallen from.

Verse 24-28 - This enigmatic description of Jacob's struggle with the angel serves as a warning that one who fights against God (rather than submitting) cannot remain un-scarred by his struggle. This point is developed in Hebrews 12:13 at the end of a section dealing with God's chastening hand.

Genesis 33

Brothers reunited and still apart

Jacob is encamped at the Jabbok river, having travelled the King's Highway that runs from Syria towards Sier. He is still 100 miles or more from his brother in Seir, yet he sees the need to send a messenger to report his return to Esau:

> *And Jacob went on his way, and the angels of God met him. And when Jacob saw them, he said, This is God's host: and he called the name of that place Mahanaim. And Jacob sent messengers before him to Esau his brother unto the land of Seir, the country of Edom. (Gen 32:1-3)*

Notice here that the record says: "the angels of God met him." Presumably, given the context, it was they who told him to call his brother.

Despite Jacob's fears for his life, Esau sees Jacob from a great distance, and runs to greet him:

> *And Esau ran to meet him, and embraced him, and fell on his neck, and kissed him: and they wept. (Gen 33:4)*

The lesson here seems to be that God desires reconciliation. It would have been so easy for Jacob to just ignore the chasm between him and Esau, hoping that he would not see him again. The better way for Jacob and his brother was for them to reconcile, and then having done so, to part on good terms to lead separate lives.

Notice that while Esau is insistent that Jacob go and live with him in Seir, Jacob agrees, yet as soon as Esau is gone ahead, he turns quietly off the King's Highway and goes to dwell in Succoth. The lesson, again, is that while we have to be on good terms where possible, we do not need to entangle ourselves in the lives of others, especially those who walk a path contrary to our own Godly way of life. Esau's path took him away from the promised land, and Jacob's path is back towards it.

> *So Esau returned that day on his way unto Seir. And Jacob journeyed to Succoth, and built him an house, and made booths for his cattle: therefore the name of the place is called Succoth. And Jacob came to Shalem, a city of Shechem,* **which is in the land of Canaan,** *when he came from Padanaram; and pitched his tent before the city. (Gen 33:16-18)*

We don't have a choice in who our family are. We may not get on with them so well. Yet God desires that we come together to make peace, and then if necessary, leave to go our separate ways.

Food for thought

Verse 4 - The way in which Esau ran to meet Jacob is echoed in the language of the parable of the prodigal son – Luke 15:20

Verse 5 - When Jacob meets Esau he explains that God has given him the things that he has. Esau, it would seem, had little time for the things of God, nevertheless Jacob still provided the explanation. Surely we would do well to imitate him. The fact that one we speak with may not believe in the God of Israel is no reason not to express our beliefs though I suspect we are shy at times of doing this for fear of ridicule.

Genesis 34

Be ye separate, saith the Lord

Notice that Hamor puts a positive slant on the potential marriage of Shechem and Dinah.

And ye shall dwell with us: and the land shall be before you; dwell and trade ye therein, and get you possessions therein. (Gen 34:10)

When the brothers reply, they add one important thing, showing they understand the implication of the marriage full well:

Then will we give our daughters unto you, and we will take your daughters to us, and we will dwell with you, and we will become one people. (Gen 34:16)

This is specifically what God did not want, a thing we learn right from the time before the flood:

And it came to pass, when men began to multiply on the face of the earth, and daughters were born unto them, That the sons of

> *God saw the daughters of men that they were fair; and they took them wives of all which they chose. And the LORD said, My spirit shall not always strive with man, for that he also is flesh: yet his days shall be an hundred and twenty years. (Gen 6:1-3)*

This pronouncement that the flood would come in 120 years time, was as a direct result of God understanding the significance of His people marrying the "daughters of men". The same phrase is used in our chapter, showing us that these events are linked:

> *And Dinah the daughter of Leah, which she bare unto Jacob, went out to see **the daughters of the land**. (Gen 34:1)*

The lesson for us, in this chapter and the preceding ones, is that the choice of wife for our sons is a critical one. We are shown in each generation (Abraham, Isaac, Jacob, Dinah) the struggle these Godly people had with the temptation to marry outside of the people of God. This struggle still goes on now. How seriously are we taking these lessons in our day?

> *Be ye not unequally yoked together with unbelievers: for what fellowship hath righteousness with unrighteousness? and what communion hath light with darkness? And what concord hath Christ with Belial? or what part hath he that believeth with an infidel? And what agreement hath the temple of God with idols? for ye are the temple of the living God; as God hath said, I will dwell in them, and walk in them; and I will be their God, and they shall be my people. Wherefore come out from among them, and be ye separate, saith the Lord, and touch not the unclean thing; and I will receive you, And will be a Father unto you, and ye shall be my sons and daughters, saith the Lord Almighty. (2Co 6:14-18)*

Food for thought

Verse 1 - Simeon and Levi were Dinah's natural brothers – they shared the same mother – Gen 35:23

Verse 13 - Jacob had been a "deceiver" (Gen 27:12), using guile at times in his life. Perhaps his sons learnt this skill from his example? When they spoke to Shechem and his father they spoke "with guile". We do well to remember that our children learn by watching us. The opposite is said of Jesus (1Pet 2:22).

Genesis 35

Bible echoes

If I asked you to name a heavily pregnant woman in the Bible, traveling to Bethlehem, you'd probably say "Mary". But Rachel took this journey long before Mary, and died in childbirth along the way. I wonder whether Mary worried about her own journey once she had heard the story of her ancestor?

> And they journeyed from Bethel; and there was but a little way to come to Ephrath: and Rachel travailed, and she had hard labour. ... And Rachel died, and was buried in the way to Ephrath, which is Bethlehem. (Gen 35:16, 19)

The beginning of idolatry - Rachel's mistake

Jacob is afraid of the people of the land, and knows that he will only be safe if God cares for him. He calls to mind his deliverance from Esau, that God had looked after him on that occasion, and resolves to cleanse his family so that they might be more pleasing to the LORD:

> Then Jacob said unto his household, and to all that were with him,

> *Put away the strange gods that are among you, and be clean, and change your garments: And let us arise, and go up to Bethel; and I will make there an altar unto God,* **who answered me in the day of my distress**, *and was with me in the way which I went. And they gave unto Jacob all the strange gods which were in their hand, and all their earrings which were in their ears; and Jacob hid them under the oak which was by Shechem. (Gen 35:2-4)*

But how is it that Jacob's household already had foreign gods among them? Had these come with the women and children of Shechem, which they had taken as a spoil from the Shechemites, along with all their possessions?

> *The sons of Jacob came upon the slain, and spoiled the city, because they had defiled their sister ... And all their wealth, and all their little ones, and their wives took they captive, and spoiled even all that was in the house. (Gen 34:27, 29)*

Possibly. But this isn't the place the Bible tells us they obtained them. There is another place where it does specifically say so. Remember the incident where Rachel carried off Laban's idols? Could it be that they still had those?

> *And Laban went to shear his sheep: and Rachel had stolen the images that were her father's. (Gen 31:19)*

Jacob had made a terrible promise to Laban that day, not knowing that Rachel had taken his idols:

> *With whomsoever thou findest thy gods, let him not live: before our brethren discern thou what is thine with me, and take it to*

thee. For Jacob knew not that Rachel had stolen them. (Gen 31:32)

Laban made a search for the idols, but didn't find them, so that Rachel was spared. Yet, now in our chapter, in the context of this purge of the "strange gods" that Jacob made, Rachel indeed dies in the very next journey they take. So the words of Jacob came true. In a terrible irony, as Jacob cleanses his house of idols, the one by whom this idolatry entered their house is removed too.

Jacob was inheritor of the promises to Abraham. Jacob was a man to whom God had appeared several times. He was man whom had been given messages by God directly. This is similar to Abraham, and Abraham in scripture is called a prophet:

Now therefore restore the man his wife; for [Abraham] is a prophet, and he shall pray for thee, and thou shalt live: and if thou restore her not, know thou that thou shalt surely die, thou, and all that are thine. (Gen 20:7)

Could it be that, perhaps unbeknownst to Jacob, his words, as the words of a prophet, came to pass?

Food for thought

Verse 4 - Jacob owned a parcel of ground at Shechem (Gen 33:19). So the gold was possibly buried on his own land, which he now had to leave.

Verse 10 - This is the second time that Jacob's name was changed to Israel (see Gen 32:28). So the name conferred by the angel after the struggle is confirmed by God Himself.

Genesis 36

Brothers of promise

Once again we see the promises being fulfilled, in that God has blessed the two sons of Isaac so greatly, that there is now insufficient room for them both in the land:

And Esau took his wives, and his sons, and his daughters, and all the persons of his house, and his cattle, and all his beasts, and all his substance, which he had got in the land of Canaan; and went into the country from the face of his brother Jacob. For their riches were more than that they might dwell together; and the land wherein they were strangers could not bear them because of their cattle. Thus dwelt Esau in mount Seir: Esau is Edom. (Gen 36:6-8)

The LORD God is clearly blessing Esau, as He is Jacob, notwithstanding the promises now rest with Jacob's descendants only. It is a little known fact that, just as Israel were later brought out of Egypt into their promised land, so Esau's descendants were given a land:

Meddle not with them; for I will not give you of their land, no, not

> so much as a foot breadth; because I have given mount Seir unto Esau for a possession. ... The Horims also dwelt in Seir beforetime; but the children of Esau succeeded them, when they had destroyed them from before them, and dwelt in their stead; as Israel did unto the land of his possession, which the LORD gave unto them. (Deu 2:5, 12)

This nation, descended from Abraham, seems to have carried on the traditions of Abraham for a time. In the book of Job, we come across a man, Eliphaz, one of Job's wise friends. Could it be that he is the same man as Esau's firstborn?

> These are the names of Esau's sons; Eliphaz the son of Adah the wife of Esau, Reuel the son of Bashemath the wife of Esau. And the sons of **Eliphaz** were **Teman**, Omar, Zepho, and Gatam, and Kenaz. (Gen 36:10-11)

The further evidence for this is that Eliphaz in Job is called a "Temanite", possibly a reference to his son?

> Now when Job's three friends heard of all this evil that was come upon him, they came every one from his own place; **Eliphaz the Temanite**, and Bildad the Shuhite, and Zophar the Naamathite: for they had made an appointment together to come to mourn with him and to comfort him. (Job 2:11)

So either Eliphaz in the book of Job is the son of Esau, or at least his descendant via Teman.

Food for thought

Verse 6 - In leaving Canaan and going "from the face of" Jacob to the East, Esau is compared with Cain, who went east to be hid from the "face" of God (Gen 4:14,16).

Verse 43 - This genealogy lays out the generations of Esau marking the point that this section was written long after the days of Esau. The family tree is replicated in 1Chron 1:35, and is not simply a list of names. It provides the background for later scriptural comments about the nation of Edom.

Genesis 37

Open rebuke is better than concealed hatred

Was Joseph naive, or even stupid? Didn't he know that his brothers hated him, and yet he still persisted in telling them about his dreams.

Actually, I don't think he was either of those things. Instead, it was the brothers who were so good at concealing their hatred. Notice that Jacob had no idea either, because he sent Joseph out into the middle of nowhere to find them, on his own:

> *And he said to him, Go, I pray thee, see whether it be well with thy brethren, and well with the flocks; and bring me word again. So he sent him out of the vale of Hebron, and he came to Shechem. (Gen 37:14)*

Jesus' lesson about concealed hatred is that it is the beginning of murder:

> *Ye have heard that it was said by them of old time, Thou shalt not kill; and whosoever shall kill shall be in danger of the judgment: But I say unto you, That whosoever is angry with his brother*

> *without a cause shall be in danger of the judgment: and whosoever shall say to his brother, Raca, shall be in danger of the council: but whosoever shall say, Thou fool, shall be in danger of hell fire. (Mat 5:21-22)*

It's like a seed which grows larger the more it is kept buried in the mind's fertile soil :

> *But every man is tempted, when he is drawn away of his own lust, and enticed. Then when lust hath conceived, it bringeth forth sin: and sin, when it is finished, bringeth forth death. (Jas 1:14-15)*

This is what happened with the brothers and their envy of Joseph. It started with envy of the coat their father gave him:

> *And his brethren envied him; but his father observed the saying. (Gen 37:11)*

In contrast to the behaviour of the brothers, their father displayed the correct attitude to Joseph's insulting dream: he rebuked him!

> *And he told it to his father, and to his brethren: and his father rebuked him, and said unto him, What is this dream that thou hast dreamed? Shall I and thy mother and thy brethren indeed come to bow down ourselves to thee to the earth? (Gen 37:10)*

As the Proverb says "Open rebuke is better than secret love", and it is obvious from the context that the proverb is speaking of hatred, concealed by a pretence of love:

> *Wrath is cruel, and anger is outrageous; but who is able to stand*

before envy? Open rebuke is better than secret love. Faithful are the wounds of a friend; but the kisses of an enemy are deceitful. (Pro 27:4-6)

Notice how Jacob and his grandfather Abraham both used open rebuke (Gen 21:25, 31:36).

*And Abraham reproved Abimelech because of a well of water, which Abimelech's servants had violently taken away. (Gen 21:25)
And Jacob was wroth, and chode with Laban: and Jacob answered and said to Laban, What is my trespass? what is my sin, that thou hast so hotly pursued after me? (Gen 31:36)*

The account of Joseph is not just a story. It is a vital lesson on which the law and gospel are built. In order to prevent hatred, we must rebuke:

Thou shalt not hate thy brother in thine heart: thou shalt in any wise rebuke thy neighbour, and not suffer sin upon him. Thou shalt not avenge, nor bear any grudge against the children of thy people, but thou shalt love thy neighbour as thyself: I am the LORD. (Lev 19:17-18)

Food for thought

Verse 8 - This reaction of the brothers is seen in the parables of Jesus (Luke 19:14,27). What was Jesus trying to say by referring the listeners back to the history of Joseph?

Verse 18 - In conspiring to kill Joseph we have a pattern set for the way that Israel would treat Jesus (Matt 21:38, Luke 20:14). Jesus and Joseph were faithful to their respective fathers, hence the hatred of the other sons.

Genesis 38

Judah, the prodigal son

In previous chapters we have seen the lengths that Abraham, Isaac, and Jacob went to, to find wives who were not of the wicked Canaanite people. This has been a struggle and a trial of faith for each of them. We have seen how Esau gave in and married two Canaanite women, and now we see Judah doing the same. Only Judah goes an extra step: he moves away from his family to dwell among the people of the land:

> *And it came to pass at that time, that Judah went down from his brethren, and turned in to a certain Adullamite, whose name was Hirah. And Judah saw there a daughter of a certain Canaanite, whose name was Shuah; and he took her, and went in unto her.* (Gen 38:1-2)

Of all those who willingly departed from the patriarchs, and therefore the promises, Judah's actions were possibly the worst. Yet only Judah repented and returned. Notice that by the time of the famine at the time of Joseph, the brothers are all back together again (Joseph is in Egypt and Benjamin with Jacob, making twelve):

> *And Joseph's **ten brethren** went down to buy corn in Egypt. (Gen 42:3)*

Esau and Lot could presumably have returned, but didn't. Judah is a singular example to us of humility and repentance. He is the prodigal son of Jesus's famous parable. He did some terrible things, but turned round, and after his conversion, became the chief tribe of Israel, through whose line Jesus was later born.

> *Judah, thou art he whom thy brethren shall praise: thy hand shall be in the neck of thine enemies; thy father's children shall bow down before thee ... The sceptre shall not depart from Judah, nor a lawgiver from between his feet. (Gen 49:8, 10)*

Food for thought

Verse 12, 20 - It seems that the use of the term "friend" conveys more than we normally mean when we use the term today. Probably it indicates a particular relationship — a man who was given a specific position to represent the man he was "friend" to. See also Judg 14:20 "used as his friend".

Verse 29-30 - Pharez and Zarah are ancestors respectively of Salmon and Achan in the book of Joshua. They doubtless were the two spies who were delivered by Rahab. Salmon then fathered Boaz. Achan, on the other hand, was more concerned with the gold.

Genesis 39

Being allied with those who had the promises

Potiphar noticed that the LORD was with Joseph:

> *And his master saw that the LORD was with him, and that the LORD made all that he did to prosper in his hand. (Gen 39:3)*

The same happened with the captain of the prison:

> *The keeper of the prison looked not to any thing that was under his hand; because the LORD was with him, and that which he did, the LORD made it to prosper. (Gen 39:23)*

It is a similar statement to when Laban noticed Jacob:

> *And Laban said unto him, I pray thee, if I have found favour in thine eyes, tarry: for I have learned by experience that the LORD hath blessed me for thy sake. (Gen 30:27)*

And when the lord of the Philistines noticed Isaac:

> *And they said, We saw certainly that the LORD was with thee: and we said, Let there be now an oath betwixt us, even betwixt us and thee, and let us make a covenant with thee; (Gen 26:28)*

The pattern is clear. Gentiles who ally themselves closely with those who have the promises, are in turn themselves blessed through those promises. Laban, by benefitting from Jacob; Potiphar, by benefitting from Joseph. And the philistine shows us the way we too ought to react; by making a covenant. The good news is that we can:

> *And the scripture, foreseeing that God would justify the heathen through faith, preached before the gospel unto Abraham, saying, In thee shall all nations be blessed. So then they which be of faith are blessed with faithful Abraham. (Gal 3:8-9)*

Food for thought

Verse 2 - Whilst "the Lord was with Joseph" we should not think that Joseph thought things were going well with him all the time he was in Egypt, for even when he was in a position of authority beyond his wildest dreams, he named his son "causing to forget" (Genesis 41:51) as a reminder of his sorrow.

Verse 18-20 - Joseph clearly made no defence of his position. He "suffered wrong" thus manifesting a meek spirit which should allow us to be defrauded, rather than seeking our own defence (see 1Cor 6:7).

Genesis 40

Extraordinary dreams for ordinary people

This chapter teaches us that prophetic dreams are not just confined to a special few, but that anyone can experience them if God so pleases.

And they dreamed a dream both of them, each man his dream in one night, each man according to the interpretation of his dream, the butler and the baker of the king of Egypt, which were bound in the prison. (Gen 40:5)

The butler and baker were just ordinary people. Perhaps highly skilled and the top of their profession, but nevertheless ordinary. They were also Egyptians, and (we assume) knew nothing of the God of Abraham, Isaac and Jacob. Laban, who meant Jacob harm, even had a dream warning him:

It is in the power of my hand to do you hurt: but the God of your father spake unto me yesternight, saying, Take thou heed that thou speak not to Jacob either good or bad. (Gen 31:29)

The idolatrous kings of Babylon had them:

The king answered and said to Daniel, whose name was Belteshazzar, Art thou able to make known unto me the dream which I have seen, and the interpretation thereof? (Dan 2:26)

We have similar occurrences of dreams in the new testament too, for example where pilot's wife was warned regarding Jesus:

When he was set down on the judgment seat, his wife sent unto him, saying, Have thou nothing to do with that just man: for I have suffered many things this day in a dream because of him. (Mat 27:19)

So we can see that prophetic dreams are widespread and can be given to anyone, at any time. We may ourselves receive such dreams, and it is up to us whether we search the scriptures to find the meaning of it. Dreams are a method God uses to instruct us:

In a dream, in a vision of the night, when deep sleep falleth upon men, in slumberings upon the bed; Then he openeth the ears of men, and sealeth their instruction, (Job 33:15-16)

Food for thought

Verse 6-7 - In noting that the prisoners (the butler and baker) were sad, Joseph is going beyond the responsibilities of a jailer. He is implementing the principles of the law of Moses (Lev 19:18) long before it was ever voiced.

Verse 15 - In saying that he was "stolen away" from his own land does not actually reflect what really happened. His own brothers sold him – though Joseph does not say that. He leaves the matter for God to judge. How often do we feel the need to spell things out in a way which does not reflect well on our brethren? Maybe we should take a leaf out of Joseph's book.

Genesis 41

Faith is the substance of things hoped for

Seven years is a long time to wait for a disaster promised in a dream, especially when you are newcomer telling everyone else what to do to prepare for it:

> *And he gathered up all the food of the seven years, which were in the land of Egypt, and laid up the food in the cities: the food of the field, which was round about every city, laid he up in the same. And Joseph gathered corn as the sand of the sea, very much, until he left numbering; for it was without number. (Gen 41:48-49)*

But Joseph kept his faith and continued to store up grain that whole time. This is a good example of what faith is: "The substance of things hoped for". The stored grain was the physical evidence (substance) of the famine to come (hoped for).

> *Now faith is the substance of things hoped for, the evidence of things not seen. (Heb 11:1)*

Thus we can see that hope, in this context, is agnostic of whether the future event is good or bad. The "hope" is that God will perform what He has promised. Thus Joseph hoped for the fulfilment of the dream that the LORD God had interpreted through him:

> *And they said unto him, We have dreamed a dream, and there is no interpreter of it. And Joseph said unto them, Do not interpretations belong to God? tell me them, I pray you. (Gen 40:8)*
>
> *And Joseph answered Pharaoh, saying, It is not in me: God shall give Pharaoh an answer of peace. (Gen 41:16)*

We can see that the dreams were prophetic, and Joseph saw them as such. Joseph is commended in Hebrews for his faith:

> *By faith Joseph, when he died, made mention of the departing of the children of Israel; and gave commandment concerning his bones. (Heb 11:22)*

The point is that God, in His foreknowledge, had planned a famine that would cause His people Israel to go into captivity according to the promises He had given to Abraham. Thus by understanding this future, and submitting to it, Joseph was able to be a tool in God's hand for ultimate good.

> *Moreover he called for a famine upon the land: he brake the whole staff of bread. He sent a man before them, even Joseph, who was sold for a servant: Whose feet they hurt with fetters: he was laid in iron: Until the time that his word came: the word of the LORD tried him. The king sent and loosed him; even the ruler of the people, and let him go free. (Psa 105:16-20)*

Food for thought

Verse 1 - So two years pass, and Joseph languishes in prison, but still believes in his God. The time is coming when Joseph who has been "tried" by the word of God (Psalm 105:19) is to move to the next stage of his work of delivering his brethren.

Verse 46 - In saying that Joseph was 30 when he stood before Pharaoh, the record has him starting his work of the salvation of his people at the same age that Jesus started his ministry (Luke 3:23) and David his reign (2Sam 5:4).

Genesis 42

Unstable as water

Reuben was Jacob's oldest son. He should have been the one allowed to safeguard Benjamin. But Jacob doesn't listen to Reuben:

> *And Reuben spake unto his father, saying, Slay my two sons, if I bring him not to thee: deliver him into my hand, and I will bring him to thee again. And he said, My son shall not go down with you; for his brother is dead, and he is left alone: if mischief befall him by the way in the which ye go, then shall ye bring down my gray hairs with sorrow to the grave. (Gen 42:37-38)*

Later Jacob says of his eldest son, "you are as unstable as water":

> *Unstable as water, thou shalt not excel; because thou wentest up to thy father's bed; then defiledst thou it: he went up to my couch. (Gen 49:4)*

Jacob felt he couldn't entrust the life of his youngest son to Reuben. After all, Joseph had been lost during his watch, and he didn't even know about it. Where was he when it happened?

> *And Reuben returned unto the pit; and, behold, Joseph was not in the pit; and he rent his clothes. (Gen 37:29)*

Judah was the one who was there to save Joseph:

> *And Judah said unto his brethren, What profit is it if we slay our brother, and conceal his blood? Come, and let us sell him to the Ishmeelites, and let not our hand be upon him; for he is our brother and our flesh. And his brethren were content. (Gen 37:26-27 KJV)*

So when later Judah steps forward and makes effectively the same offer, Jacob listens:

> *And Judah said unto Israel his father, Send the lad with me, and we will arise and go; that we may live, and not die, both we, and thou, and also our little ones. I will be surety for him; of my hand shalt thou require him: if I bring him not unto thee, and set him before thee, then let me bear the blame for ever: For except we had lingered, surely now we had returned this second time. And their father Israel said unto them, If it must be so now, do this; take of the best fruits in the land in your vessels, and carry down the man a present, a little balm, and a little honey, spices, and myrrh, nuts, and almonds: (Gen 43:8-11)*

Judah has the authority to back up his word with actions, whereas Reuben doesn't. On his death bed, Jacob says this of Judah:

> *Judah, thou art he whom thy brethren shall praise: thy hand shall be in the neck of thine enemies; thy father's children shall bow*

down before thee. (Gen 49:8)

These words, "your father's children shall bow down to you", are the words of Joseph's dream that started these events off in the first place. Thus the dream, which spoke initially of Joseph, ultimately speaks of Judah, the man who could be trusted:

> *Moreover he refused the tabernacle of Joseph, and chose not the tribe of Ephraim: But chose the tribe of Judah, the mount Zion which he loved. (Psa 78:67-68)*

Food for thought

Verse 21 - In the comment that the brothers say one to another we begin to see their repentance for the evil that they had done to Joseph.

Verse 28 - Notice that despite their behaviour, Joseph's brothers knew that God was at work in their lives. How often we are like this. We recognise God as being all powerful but then we continue to pursue our own objectives.

Genesis 43

The sun, moon and stars

Joseph's dreams were prophetic. They spoke of the future where the sons of Jacob would bow down to their brother:

> And he dreamed yet another dream, and told it his brethren, and said, Behold, I have dreamed a dream more; and, behold, the sun and the moon and the eleven stars made obeisance to me. (Gen 37:9)

This came true when the brothers bowed down to Joseph, the ruler of Egypt who now had the power of life or death over them. Notice how deliberate the text is in pointing out this fulfilment:

> And Joseph was the governor over the land, and he it was that sold to all the people of the land: and Joseph's brethren came, and **bowed down themselves before him with their faces to the earth**. (Gen 42:6)
> And when Joseph came home, they brought him the present which was in their hand into the house, and **bowed themselves to him to the earth** ... And they answered, Thy servant our father

is in good health, he is yet alive. And they **bowed down their heads, and made obeisance.** *(Gen 43:26, 28)*

However, it was not just the 11 stars that bowed to the star in the dream. It was also the sun and the moon. Now this is where things take a curious turn. Remember that Jacob interpreted what he thought the dream meant:

And he told it to his father, and to his brethren: and his father rebuked him, and said unto him, What is this dream that thou hast dreamed? Shall I and thy mother and thy brethren indeed come to bow down ourselves to thee to the earth? (Gen 37:10)

Jacob placed himself as the sun, and Joseph's mother as the Moon, both bowing down to Joseph's star. But unlike the brothers, when he saw Joseph he didn't have time to bow, for as soon as Joseph saw him he ran and embraced him:

And Joseph made ready his chariot, and went up to meet Israel his father, to Goshen, and presented himself unto him; and he fell on his neck, and wept on his neck a good while. (Gen 46:29)

It seems, however, that at the very end of his life, Jacob remembers the dream, and in an act that must have hurt his frail body, bows himself on the bed before Joseph.

And the time drew nigh that Israel must die: and he called his son Joseph, and said unto him, If now I have found grace in thy sight, put, I pray thee, thy hand under my thigh, and deal kindly and truly with me; bury me not, I pray thee, in Egypt: But I will lie with my fathers, and thou shalt carry me out of Egypt, and bury me in their buryingplace. And he said, I will do as thou hast said. And he said, Swear unto me. And he sware unto him. And Israel bowed himself upon the bed's head. (Gen 47:29-31)

It is not until Joseph has sworn, that Jacob finally bows. This is how important it was to Jacob to have his bones buried in the promised land.

Yet Jacob has one more trick up his sleeve. It seems that though he bowed to Joseph, he was not prepared to let this prophecy pass to Joseph's children. In other words, for some reason Jacob did not feel that Joseph's descendants through Ephraim and Manasseh would be fit to rule over their brethren. It is the following event that is specifically picked up in Hebrews, in order to commend the faith of Jacob. You see, Jacob's struggle had always been down to one thing. That he loved Rachel so much that he couldn't see that she was not the wife God had chosen for him. And so in his final act he blesses Joseph's sons, and instead of bowing, makes the supreme effort of standing before them:

By faith Jacob, when he was a dying, blessed both the sons of Joseph; and worshipped, leaning upon the top of his staff. (Heb 11:21)

You see, the elephant in the room is that Joseph's mother, the moon in Jacob's interpretation of the dream, was already long dead. She never did bow down to Joseph. Jacob finally realised that his first wife, Leah, was the rightful moon. She was the woman by which the promises would be fulfilled. Like Abraham, who sent his other wives away, Jacob now realises that he must act to correct his mistake. He should not have preferred Rachel's children (Joseph and Benjamin) above Leah's children. And so in some of his final words, he transfers the prophecy of the dream away from Joseph and onto Judah, the son of Leah:

Judah, thou art he whom thy brethren shall praise: thy hand shall be in the neck of thine enemies; **thy father's children shall bow down before thee.** *(Gen 49:8)*

Food for thought

Verse 8 - Judah had interceded for Joseph (Gen 37:26) that he might save his life by selling him. Now he intercedes again offering his own son as surety.

Verse 15 - The seeming casual way in which the preparation of the sons and the taking of Benjamin is recorded hides the anguish that must have been in Jacob's mind. One wonders what the ten brothers thought, remembering that they had sold Benjamin's brother into Egypt some 10-11 years earlier. Actions always have consequences. The sons of Jacob are now learning that consequences follow on from their actions towards Joseph so long ago.

Genesis 44

Judah, the son who returned

The brothers words to Joseph's servant are very similar to Jacob's words to Laban. The situation also is similar:

> And he overtook them, and he spake unto them these same words. And they said unto him ... how then should we steal out of thy lord's house silver or gold? With whomsoever of thy servants it be found, both let him die, and we also will be my lord's bondmen. (Gen 44:6-9)

> And he took his brethren with him, and pursued after him seven days' journey; and they overtook him in the mount Gilead. ... With whomsoever thou findest thy gods, let him not live: before our brethren discern thou what is thine with me, and take it to thee. For Jacob knew not that Rachel had stolen them. (Gen 31:23, 32)

We have a pursuit, then an accusation, a denial, and in their confidence of being innocent, a judgement upon themselves. The interesting thing is that these brothers would all have been there at that first incredibly stressful event, where they fled with their father from the increasingly belligerent uncle. They would have looked on with trepidation as Laban's men searched each man's bags. They also knew that soon after Jacob uttered those words, Rachel did in fact die:

> *And as for me, when I came from Padan, Rachel died by me in the land of Canaan in the way, when yet there was but a little way to come unto Ephrath: and I buried her there in the way of Ephrath; the same is Bethlehem. (Gen 48:7)*

So when Joseph's servant revealed the gold in their sacks, they suspected that God had brought events round to this.

> *And Judah said, What shall we say unto my lord? what shall we speak? or how shall we clear ourselves? God hath found out the iniquity of thy servants: behold, we are my lord's servants, both we, and he also with whom the cup is found. (Gen 44:16)*

So Joseph had used his knowledge of the Laban event they had all experienced in their youth, to stage a similar event so that they might be accused. As a result the brothers were condemned by their own mouths.

The important thing here is to note that Joseph could have judged them at this point and taken them all into slavery. He held all the cards. And then note the crucial elements of Judah's earnest confession:

- We can't clear ourselves
- Our iniquity is clear to God
- We are your servants

Now does that ring any bells? Have we heard this elsewhere? I'll give you a further clue: remember that they were hungry and had no bread?

> *And when he came to himself, he said, How many hired servants of my father's have bread enough and to spare, and* **I perish with hunger***! I will arise and go to my father, and will say unto him, Father,* **I have sinned against heaven***, and before thee, And am no more worthy to be called thy son:* **make me as one of thy hired servants***. (Luk 15:17-19)*

Judah's conversion and confession is the model of any sinner that repents and comes to Jesus. He sinned in being part of the plot against Joseph. He left the family and wasted his time with the women of Canaan. He came back and offered to give his life to safeguard his brother. And now he is the one that confesses their sin before Joseph. Joseph, taking a role here like Jesus, forgives them.

This is why we have the chapter about Judah (chapter 38) inserted in the account of Joseph. This is why, now that the transformation of Judah is complete, it it *he* that takes the central role. Rather than being called "Jacob's sons", they are now called "Judah's brothers":

> *And Judah and his brethren came to Joseph's house; for he was yet there: and they fell before him on the ground. (Gen 44:14)*

Food for thought

Verse 14 - In falling down before Joseph the brothers are fulfilling Joseph's dream of Genesis 37:7.

Verse 24-30 - Note the repeated way in which Judah refers to Jacob as "my father". This shows deep remorse and concern for his father. The change of heart is being seen in the very way that Judah speaks. This is a lesson for us. Repentance is more than saying sorry. Repentance is seen in a changed heart which is reflected in changed speech.

Genesis 45

Joseph - a pattern of salvation in Jesus Christ

Joseph had understood all along that the challenging events of his past were there for a purpose:

> And Joseph said unto his brethren, Come near to me, I pray you. And they came near. And he said, I am Joseph your brother, whom ye sold into Egypt. Now therefore be not grieved, nor angry with yourselves, that ye sold me hither: for God did send me before you to preserve life. (Gen 45:4-5)

And in recognising this, he considered his brother's part in it as part of God's plan too:

> And God sent me before you to preserve you a posterity in the earth, and to save your lives by a great deliverance. So now **it was not you that sent me hither, but God**: and he hath made me a father to Pharaoh, and lord of all his house, and a ruler throughout all the land of Egypt. (Gen 45:7-8)

This is an amazing attitude, and one we should try to copy. If God is in control of events for our good, then why should we get angry with those who appear to hurt us along the way? It could be that in the very act of trying to hurt us, they are inadvertently doing God's will.

It is of course important for those doing the wrong to also recognise God's hand, and to repent. Peter, in the new testament, challenges to Jews for their role in slaying Jesus, telling them that this was predetermined by God, just as the actions of Joseph's brothers had been:

> *Him, being delivered by the determinate counsel and foreknowledge of God, ye have taken, and by wicked hands have crucified and slain: (Act 2:23)*

Just as Joseph was sent ahead to Egypt to save his family, so Jesus was sent ahead to save those who trust in him. Just as Joseph was pulled out of prison to a new and glorious life at the right hand of Pharaoh, so Jesus was raised from the dead to be at the right hand of God, full of glory:

> *This Jesus hath God raised up, whereof we all are witnesses. Therefore being by the right hand of God exalted, and having received of the Father the promise of the Holy Ghost, he hath shed forth this, which ye now see and hear ... Therefore let all the house of Israel know assuredly, that God hath made that same Jesus, whom ye have crucified, both Lord and Christ. (Act 2:32-33, 36)*

The reaction of the Jews who heard this is an example to us all. It mirrors the repentance of Joseph's brothers, and Joseph's willingness to forgive them:

> *Now when they heard this, they were pricked in their heart, and said unto Peter and to the rest of the apostles, Men and brethren,*

what shall we do? Then Peter said unto them, Repent, and be baptized every one of you in the name of Jesus Christ for the remission of sins, and ye shall receive the gift of the Holy Ghost. For the promise is unto you, and to your children, and to all that are afar off, even as many as the Lord our God shall call. (Act 2:37-39)

Food for thought

Verse 1 - The making known of Joseph to his brethren is a pattern of the revelation of Christ to repentant Israel. Whilst they will be horrified at what they have done to him their repentance will assure that Jesus will lovingly embrace them - and so 'all Israel shall be saved' (Romans 11:26) - of course this is not a blanket salvation. It is consequent upon repentance

Verse 6 - We are now in the second year and there are five more years of famine to come. So we are able to see where the events of Chapters 42-45 fit in. Also we know that we are 11 years on from the dreams of the butler and baker (Gen 41:1).

Genesis 46

The Mystery of the Missing Traveler

Have you ever gone on a long walk with a large group of people? You counted them up at the beginning, and at each gate in the path, did you count them again, just to be sure no-one's missing? Jacob did this. He counted the people in his traveling party:

> These be the sons of Leah, which she bare unto Jacob in Padanaram, with his daughter Dinah: all the souls of his sons and his daughters were thirty and three. ... These are the sons of Zilpah, whom Laban gave to Leah his daughter, and these she bare unto Jacob, even sixteen souls. ... These are the sons of Rachel, which were born to Jacob: all the souls were fourteen. ... And the sons of Naphtali; Jahzeel, and Guni, and Jezer, and Shillem. (Gen 46:15, 18, 22, 24)

So 33 + 16 + 14 + 4 = 67, plus Jacob, Leah, and Zilpah = 70, but subtract 3 for Joseph and his sons, who were already in Egypt = 67.

This tallies with verse 27. 70 persons, and 3 were already in Egypt, gives 67. So far, so good:

> *And the sons of Joseph, which were born him in Egypt, were two souls: all the souls of the house of Jacob, which came into Egypt, were threescore and ten. (Gen 46:27)*

But in verse 26 they've suddenly reduced to 66. One person is missing!

> *All the souls that came with Jacob into Egypt, which came out of his loins, besides Jacob's sons' wives, all the souls were threescore and six; (Gen 46:26)*

Who is the missing traveler, and what happened to them?

Food for thought

Verse 4 - Jacob's concern about going down to Egypt is allayed by God, who reminds him of the promise to Abram, to "bring thee up again," quoting Genesis 15:16. Of course Jacob did not return to the land of Israel whilst he was alive. His dead body was brought back. However God has not broken His promise. The promise to Abraham in Genesis 15:16 was looking further than Israel's time in Egypt. When God spoke to Abraham He was looking to the time of the resurrection.

Verses 8-27 - This section is, it might seem, superfluous to the narrative. One point that comes from the list of names is the degree to which God had already blessed Jacob in line with the promises that God had made to Abraham and his seed, that he would multiply them. See Genesis 17:2 for example.

Genesis 47

I will multiply you exceedingly

In this chapter we have a clue as to how the children of Israel multiplied so greatly in the land of Egypt. First of all, notice that the ordinary Egyptian citizen had sold their money, flocks and land to Pharaoh, and are now tenant farmers:

> *Wherefore shall we die before thine eyes, both we and our land? buy us and our land for bread, and we and our land will be servants unto Pharaoh: and give us seed, that we may live, and not die, that the land be not desolate ... Then Joseph said unto the people, Behold, I have bought you this day and your land for Pharaoh: lo, here is seed for you, and ye shall sow the land. And it shall come to pass in the increase, that ye shall give the fifth part unto Pharaoh, and four parts shall be your own, for seed of the field, and for your food, and for them of your households, and for food for your little ones. (Gen 47:19, 23-24)*

This they went into willingly, and were grateful for:

> *And they said, Thou hast saved our lives: let us find grace in the*

sight of my lord, and we will be Pharaoh's servants. (Gen 47:25)

Contrast the family of Jacob, who were provided for with bread by Joseph, and also had the best of the pasture land for their flocks:

And Joseph placed his father and his brethren, and gave them a possession in the land of Egypt, in the best of the land, in the land of Rameses, as Pharaoh had commanded. And Joseph nourished his father, and his brethren, and all his father's household, with bread, according to their families. (Gen 47:11-12)

This gave them a fertile seed bed from which to grow, so to speak, into a great nation:

*And Israel dwelt in the land of Egypt, in the country of Goshen; and they had possessions therein, and grew, and **multiplied exceedingly**. (Gen 47:27)*

Once again we see God's hand in bringing about the promises to Abraham, to greatly multiply his seed as the sand on the sea shore:

*And I will make my covenant between me and thee, and will **multiply thee exceedingly**. (Gen 17:2)*

But not only this, we see that God is also bringing about His commandment to Adam and Eve, and to Noah, a subject we covered in the chapter for Genesis 11:

*And God blessed Noah and his sons, and said unto them, Be fruitful, and **multiply**, and replenish the earth. (Gen 9:1)*

Food for thought

Verse 9 - Jacob describes his life as being of days which were "few and evil" however when he blessed Joseph's sons he seems to have a different thing to say (Gen 48:15) "the angel which redeemed me…" Maybe by the time he came to bless the lads he appreciated more fully how God had been working in his life.

Verse 28 - Joseph was 17 when he was sold into Egypt (Genesis 37:2) and he spends 17 years with his father in Egypt. So Joseph has two 17 year periods with his father.

Genesis 48

The extra portion

When Jacob was old, the time came to bless Joseph, and to give him his inheritance. But he didn't bless Joseph; he blessed his two sons:

> *And now thy two sons, Ephraim and Manasseh, which were born unto thee in the land of Egypt before I came unto thee into Egypt, are mine; as Reuben and Simeon, they shall be mine. (Gen 48:5)*

The blessing he gives the two boys gives Joseph an extra portion, based on the promise of God to make of Jacob a great nation:

> *And Jacob said unto Joseph, God Almighty appeared unto me at Luz in the land of Canaan, and blessed me, And said unto me, Behold, I will make thee fruitful, and multiply thee, and I will make of thee a multitude of people; and will give this land to thy seed after thee for an everlasting possession. ... The Angel which redeemed me from all evil, bless the lads; and let my name be named on them, and the name of my fathers Abraham and Isaac; and let them grow into a multitude in the midst of the earth. (Gen*

48:3-4, 16)

By doing this Jacob is elevating Ephraim and Manasseh to the same level as the rest of his sons, and because of this there are thirteen tribes in Israel, not twelve. It seems strange, because we don't hear about thirteen tribes, and the reason for this is because Levi is not counted because the Levites became the priesthood (Josh 14:4).

> *For the children of Joseph were two tribes, Manasseh and Ephraim: therefore they gave no part unto the Levites in the land, save cities to dwell in, with their suburbs for their cattle and for their substance. (Jos 14:4)*

So why did Jacob give Joseph this extra portion all of a sudden? Jacob tells Joseph this reason:

> *Moreover I have given to thee one portion above thy brethren, which I took out of the hand of the Amorite with my sword and with my bow. (Gen 48:22)*

What does he mean? The answer lies in Joshua 24:32 which recounts Joseph's burial, much later, in the land of Israel:

> *And the bones of Joseph, which the children of Israel brought up out of Egypt, buried they in Shechem, in a parcel of ground which Jacob bought of the sons of Hamor the father of Shechem for an hundred pieces of silver: and it became the inheritance of the children of Joseph. (Jos 24:32)*

This parcel of ground is what Jacob is referring to, and notice that here it states that this became Joseph's inheritance, an extra portion, just as

Jacob had said.

This is part of the land that Simeon and Levi took by force, presumably with their sword and bow, in Genesis 34.

So why is all this a big deal? It is because Joseph, the second most powerful man in Egypt, was still a slave in Egypt. He was not going to go home to the promised land. By giving this promise to Joseph, Jacob was ensuring that his son and all their descendants would have the focus of their freedom and salvation upon a plot of land in Canaan. As slaves, the one place on earth that was their own.

This extra portion of inheritance, of this piece of land, is the common thing in both Jacob and Joseph's lives that is specifically called out in Hebrews 11 as being the evidence of their faith in God:

> *By faith Jacob, when he was a dying, blessed both the sons of Joseph; and worshipped, leaning upon the top of his staff. By faith Joseph, when he died, made mention of the departing of the children of Israel; and gave commandment concerning his bones. (Heb 11:21-22)*

This plot of land was an anchor for their faith, the substance of the promises which were unseen and far away.

Food for thought

Verse 14-20 - We read of "Ephraim" often in the historical and prophetic books of scripture and possibly think nothing of a large element of the nation being named in this way. However this repeated use of "Ephraim" shows that what Jacob had said of Ephraim in the blessing actually came true. Thus Jacob was a prophet, as was his grandfather Abraham (Gen 20:7).

Verse 22 - When Israel told Joseph that God would bring him back to the land of Canaan he was basing his comments on Genesis 15:14.

Genesis 49

The prophecies of Jacob

In this chapter Jacob, now an old man, gives a prophecy for each of his sons, regarding the future of their tribe:

> *And Jacob called unto his sons, and said, Gather yourselves together, that I may tell you that which shall befall you in the last days. (Gen 49:1)*

Reuben loses his firstborn status because of his sin in sleeping with his father's concubine (Gen 35:22).

Simeon and **Levi** would be scattered in Israel because of their violence towards Shechem's family (Gen 34:25). This came to pass when the tribe of Levi was given a place in each tribe of Israel (Num 35:1-8).

Judah was to become the lead nation and from him would come the king. This was fulfilled when David became king over all the tribes of Israel, and speaks of Jesus who will reign on the throne of David:

> *And, behold, thou shalt conceive in thy womb, and bring forth a*

son, and shalt call his name JESUS. He shall be great, and shall be called the Son of the Highest: and the Lord God shall give unto him the throne of his father David: And he shall reign over the house of Jacob for ever; and of his kingdom there shall be no end. (Luk 1:31-33)

Zebulun would dwell by the sea and be privileged to obtain the first teachings of the Lord Jesus: (Judg 5:14

And leaving Nazareth, he came and dwelt in Capernaum, which is upon the sea coast, in the borders of Zabulon and Nephthalim: That it might be fulfilled which was spoken by Esaias the prophet, saying, The land of Zabulon, and the land of Nephthalim, by the way of the sea, beyond Jordan, Galilee of the Gentiles; (Mat 4:13-15)

Issachar would be a strong worker, like a donkey bearing burdens, possibly fulfilled in 1Chron 12:40.

Dan would be a serpent biting the heel, causing people to fall, which happened in Judges when they took Micah's idols (Judges 18) and the golden calf was set up there (1ki 12:28-30)

Gad was nearly destroyed by his brothers but was saved at the last minute (Josh 22:33).

Asher would provide food in abundance, fulfilled when Hezekiah kept the passover (2chr 30:11 and 31:5)

Naphtali would be like a hind, a reference to his sure feet in war (see Psalm 18:33), demonstrated in their army descending mount Tabor to fight Sisera (Judg 4:6, 14-16)

Joseph (**Ephraim** and **Manasseh**) would be two of the strongest and most influential of the tribes.

Benjamin would devour the prey and divide the spoil, fulfilled in detail Obadiah 1:17-20.

> ... *the house of Jacob shall possess their possessions. And the house of Jacob shall be a fire, and the house of Joseph a flame, and the house of Esau for stubble, and they shall kindle in them, and **devour** them ... And they of the south shall possess the mount of Esau; and they of the plain the Philistines: and they shall possess the fields of Ephraim, and the fields of Samaria: and **Benjamin shall possess Gilead**. And the captivity of this host of the children of Israel shall possess that of the Canaanites, even unto Zarephath; and the captivity of Jerusalem, which is in Sepharad, shall possess the cities of the south. (Oba 1:17-20)*

Food for thought

Verse 9 - In speaking of Judah as a "lion's whelp" we have the origin of the idea that Jesus uses in Revelation 5:5.

Verse 29 - Jacob's desire to be buried in the land of Canaan shows his firm conviction that the promises to him and his fathers will be fulfilled. He identified with the land of Canaan rather than the land of Egypt.

Genesis 50

Bring forth My armies

Why was it was necessary for the children of Israel to go into the land of Egypt? Because of the iniquity of the people of Canaan among whom they had dwelled:

> And he said unto Abram, Know of a surety that thy seed shall be a stranger in a land that is not theirs, and shall serve them; and they shall afflict them four hundred years; And also that nation, whom they shall serve, will I judge: and afterward shall they come out with great substance. And thou shalt go to thy fathers in peace; thou shalt be buried in a good old age. But in the fourth generation they shall come hither again: **for the iniquity of the Amorites is not yet full.** (Gen 15:13-16)

There was no way for Israel to grow in size in the land of Canaan, since this would bring them into constant conflict with the residents. Instead, God promised Abraham that his children would go into a foreign land (Egypt) for four hundred years, and then come out with "great substance". The reason given is:

for the iniquity of the Amorites is not yet full.

Remember that Abraham, Isaac and Jacob had lived among these people, and some of them God had judged (Sodom and Gomorrah), but some of them they had lived alongside in peace:

> *And there came one that had escaped, and told Abram the Hebrew; for he dwelt in the plain of Mamre the Amorite, brother of Eshcol, and brother of Aner: and **these were confederate with Abram**. (Gen 14:13)*

So even though God had promised the whole of that land to Abraham and his descendants, it would not have been right to push out the people who lived there currently. In speaking of the iniquity of the Amorites in Genesis 15:16, God is saying that a time will come when their iniquity is so great, that He would have to judge them and remove them, as he did with Sodom. Yet rather than using fire and brimstone, He would use the now greatly enlarged people of Israel to do it. In other words, God was creating a nation for Himself who would replace the wicked Amorites, and an army to take them on.

These same promises to Abraham are quoted in Exodus when God brings Israel out of Egypt, and note how the children of Israel are now called "Mine armies":

> *But Pharaoh shall not hearken unto you, that I may lay my hand upon Egypt, **and bring forth Mine armies**, and My people the children of Israel, out of the land of Egypt by great judgments. (Exo 7:4)*

Joseph knew this, and that the time determined (400 years) was greater than his own generation. He was happy to submit to the will of God and remain in that land, knowing that it was in Egypt that God was preserving them, and that in generations to come God would act as He had promised:

> *And Joseph said unto his brethren, I die: and God will surely visit you, and bring you out of this land unto the land which he sware to Abraham, to Isaac, and to Jacob. (Gen 50:24)*

Food for thought

Verse 16-18 - It is 17 years since Joseph made himself known to his brethren but now their father is dead they still are concerned that Joseph will treat them roughly. They did not understand what full forgiveness after repentance really means. We run the risk of being like the brothers. Our God is willing to forgive us if we are repentant - however, do we still wonder?

Verse 20-21 - Israel murdered Jesus, yet he will return to be their saviour, and they will recognise him at long last. God meant that for good also. The death of Jesus was determined by God (see Acts 2:23). Thus Joseph is a pattern of how God would save His people by one man who would suffer for them.

Epilogue

And so the first book of the Bible finishes, with Joseph giving command concerning his bones, by faith in the promises given to Abraham so many generations before. We too are able to trust in the promises to Abraham, since they spoke ultimately of Jesus Christ, the descendant of Abraham who would be "the seed" mentioned in those promises:

> *Now to Abraham and his seed were the promises made. He saith not, And to seeds, as of many; but as of one, And to thy seed, which is Christ. ... But the scripture hath concluded all under sin, that the promise by faith of Jesus Christ might be given to them that believe.* (Gal 3:16, 22)

We are able to be counted as the seed of Abraham, and heirs according to the promise, if we have faith in Jesus Christ. This Jesus is patterned on Joseph who went into Egypt and suffered for the saving of his whole family, and when they came to him, he nourished them and forgave all their sins.

In Genesis we have built a foundation of knowledge as to how God expects us to act, not to be envious as Cain was, not to disobey as Adam and Eve did, and perhaps the subject given most space in the pages of this first book, how to choose a life partner who is compatible with our faith.

Genesis lays the foundation for all the rest of scripture, both the Old and New Testament, and if we go on to read the next 65 books, we will see constant reference and allusions to this magnificent book. Genesis therefore is truly the starting point of the world, of God's plan, and also of our knowledge of Him and His purpose, eventually fully revealed in His son, the Lord Jesus Christ.

Other books in the series

If you have enjoyed *Food for thought in Genesis* then why not sign up for news about other books in the series?

The *Food for thought in the Old Testament* series aims to build up into a library of books covering each chapter in the Old Testament of the Bible.

Sign up here for publication announcements and exclusive offers: www.woodland.press/sign-up

Genesis ✓	Joshua	Ezra, Nehemiah & Esther	Jeremiah & Lamentations
Exodus	Judges & Ruth	Job	Ezekiel
Leviticus	1 & 2 Samuel	Psalms	Daniel & Hosea
Numbers	1 & 2 Kings	Proverbs, Ecclesiastes & Song of Solomon	Joel to Nahum
Deuteronomy	1 & 2 Chronicles	Isaiah	Habakkuk to Malachi

About the Author

Rob de Jongh is a lifelong Bible student and has been sharing his perspective on the Bible through talks, studies and group work for the last 20 years. He has written over one thousand Bible studies and has become known for his fresh perspective, accessible writing style, and ability to make the Bible relevant. He formerly worked as a non-fiction editor alongside some of the world's best educators, and helped to devise bestselling books for two successive publishers. Catch up with him at www.woodland.press

www.ingramcontent.com/pod-product-compliance
Lightning Source LLC
Chambersburg PA
CBHW071621080526
44588CB00010B/1217